Redefining
Your
LIFE
D.I.E.T.

Advance Praise

"If I've heard one thing repeatedly in my decades of work with executive women, it's the false idea that women must put self-care low on their priority list. In her refreshing new book, *Redefining Your Life D.I.E.T.*, Dr. Sheila Robinson not only refutes that idea, she explains how prioritizing self-care leads not only to greater well-being but to maximum productivity in every role in life. If you are a woman who juggles multiple roles, you can't afford to miss this book."

—**Dr. Rosina L. Racioppi**, President and CEO, WOMEN Unlimited

"Dr. Sheila Robinson is a leader, a believer, and a role model for women and girls across the country. I love her integrity and easy-to-follow advice. Her concept of D.I.E.T. is transformative and inspirational. To be your best self, Dr. Robinson lays out a plan and framework that is both doable and sustainable. This is the book to obtain and share to be our best healthy selves. Transform your thinking and your actions to make the biggest impact in your life. Job well done, Dr. Robinson."

—**Darlene Slaughter**, VP, Chief Diversity Officer, March of Dimes

"All too often people sacrifice their self-care due to the perception of being selfish. As Dr. Sheila Robinson shares her personal, passionate, and successful—yet humble—journey, she lays out a foundation of wellness and challenges you to explore making positive changes in your life. Each chapter holds a collection of powerful resources to move from 'what if?' to 'change is here now.' With easy tips and reminders for how to be aware of what you need through her D.I.E.T. (Drink-Intake-Exercise-Think) approach, Dr. Sheila reminds you that if you are open to transformation, you can achieve the mind and body you deserve."

—**Erin Tselenchuk**, Co-Founder and Co-CEO, RISEQUITY

"Thank you, Dr. Robinson, for reminding us that when it comes to changing our nutritional habits, it isn't about making huge leaps and strides; it's about making small, sustainable changes that have a long-lasting impact. The last year has not only been polarizing on a number of fronts; it has also served as a reminder that prioritizing our health—in all areas—should be goal number one. We can't help others if we aren't helping ourselves. Thank you for this important resource."

—**Jackie Glenn**, CEO and Founder,
Glenn Diversity Inclusion & HR Solutions

"Dr. Robinson's book *Redefining Your D.I.E.T.: Transform How You Look, Feel, and Perform* is so timely as the pandemic brought health to the forefront of many conversations. During COVID-19, I was caring for family members in high-risk categories. Due to stress, combined with a bad habit of mindless eating and drinking, I gained a lot of weight. Many women who were working at kitchen tables, plus caring for young children, gained weight too. I like that this book focuses on lifestyle changes—small adjustments that could become habits—as opposed to short-term restrictive diets that are not sustainable."

—**Ria Stern**, Principal,
ASLK Associates

"Dr. Sheila Robinson has, for many years, inspired thousands of women from many diverse backgrounds. Her messages are always timely, relevant, and practical. *Redefining Your D.I.E.T.* is another example of Sheila helping women to their fullest. The personal stories and research combine for a great balance to feed the heart and the head. This book is for all women everywhere."

—**Mary-Frances Winters**, President and CEO,
The Winters Group, Inc.

Redefining Your **LIFE** D.I.E.T.

Transform How You *Look, Feel,* and *Perform*

Sheila Robinson, EdD
Foreword by Dr. Michelle Robin

Redefining Your Life D.I.E.T.

Transform How You Look, Feel, and Perform

© 2021 Sheila Robinson, EdD

Disclaimer: The publisher and the author make no representations or warranties with respect to the accuracy or completeness of the contents of this work and specifically disclaim all warranties, including without limitation warranties of fitness for a particular purpose. No warranty may be created or extended by sales or promotional materials. The strategies contained herein may not be suitable for every situation. This work is sold with the understanding that neither the author nor publisher is engaged in rendering medical, legal, accounting, or other professional services. If professional assistance is required, the services of a competent professional person should be sought. Neither the publisher nor the author shall be liable for damages arising herefrom. The fact that an organization or website is referred to in this work as a citation and/or a potential source of further information does not mean that the author or the publisher endorses the information the organization or website may provide or recommendations it may make. Further, readers should be aware that internet websites listed in this work might have changed or disappeared between the time this work was written and the time it is read.

To contact the author, Sheila Robinson, visit

- Website: https://www.diversitywoman.com/
- LinkedIn: https://www.linkedin.com/in/dr-sheila-robinson-0318294/
- Facebook: https://www.facebook.com/DiversityWomanMagazine/
- Twitter: https://twitter.com/DrSheila

To contact the publisher, Gravitas Press, visit www.GravitasPress.com

ISBN: 978-1-7359435-3-4

Content coach and publisher: Bonnie Budzowski
Book strategist: Leslie A. Rubin
Author photo: FabioCamara.com
Cover & Interior Design by: Melissa Farr, melissa@backporchcreative.com

*This book is dedicated to every woman
who wants to transform her life and
become her personal and professional best.*

Table of Contents

Acknowledgments — xi

Foreword — xiii

Chapter 1 My Story: What I Didn't Know Could Kill Me — 1

Chapter 2 Refreshing News: What Diet Is Not — 9

Chapter 3 Essential Foundation: Mindset — 21

Chapter 4 Creating Space for Success: Self-care — 31

Chapter 5 Enemy Number One: Stress — 43

Chapter 6 Hydration Is Health: Drink — 57

Chapter 7 You Are What You Eat, and More: Intake — 67

Chapter 8 Enjoy How You Move: Exercise — 81

Chapter 9 Tending Your Mental Garden: Think — 95

Chapter 10 Refresh and Restore: Sleep — 111

Chapter 11 Tie It Together: Celebrate Results — 121

Resources for You at Diversity Woman Media — *135*

About the Author — *136*

Sources Cited — *139*

Acknowledgments

I would like to acknowledge and thank a number of people who helped make this book a reality.

First, my daughter, Leah Robinson, and my mother, Mildred Thomas. The love I have for you propels me each day and has even more so as I set out on the journey to write this book. While I am accountable to myself, I feel even more responsible to be healthy for you.

My loving sisters, Darlene Crawford and Sharon Cunningham. You encourage and inspire me daily. You mean so much to me, and I am grateful you are in my corner.

My friends. You were such a big part of my inspiration to write this book. So many of you have told me that I am helping you in all areas of your life. Please know that you have helped me too. On more than one occasion, friends have told me that when one aspect of their lives was less than whole or congruent, the other aspects of their lives were out of whack too. I found that health, wellness, and self-care are key. When I made self-care a priority, everything else fell into place. My leadership productivity and the value I have added to Diversity Woman Media have skyrocketed since. I thank you for finding value in my research and personal journey, which I am sharing with you in this book.

My team at Diversity Woman Media. While I have a zillion ideas daily and probably make you crazy, you are my grounding force. Your belief in me and the direction I have set for us is what keeps us innovating. Your embrace of what we do is for the success of all women. I appreciate and respect all of you more than words can express.

My publisher and my book strategist, Bonnie Budzowski and Leslie A. Rubin, respectively. Your team approach to book writing, your skills and guidance on the process, along with drive, made this book something I'm proud to unveil today. I needed your expertise to turn my ideas and voice into magic that the reader would receive and value.

Contributors: A special thank you to those who shared their time, expertise, and experiences to enrich this book: Edwina Baskin-Bey, MD, Michael Breus, PhD, Shaun Canoy, Johnnetta B. Cole, PhD, Michelle Emebo, MPH, CCRP, Shanequa Fleming, EdD, Nancy O'Reilly, PsyD, Mindy Pelz, DC, Michelle Robin, DC, Janet Taylor, MD, and Rena Vokoun, MS.

As they say, it takes a village. I could not have completed this project without all of you.

A final note to my readers: If I can do it, you can do it. It's your turn, I am here cheering YOU on!

Foreword

My job as a chiropractor and founder of Your Wellness Connection is to help people make the most of their life minutes. For thirty-plus years, I have been helping my clients create healthy habits, one small change at a time. I don't believe in crash diets or fleeting health trends that encourage deprivation or shame. And I know change doesn't have to be difficult or dramatic to be meaningful.

That is why the book you are holding in your hands is so important. It's a combination of one woman's inspirational story of gradual but lasting change—with lessons, tips, and manageable steps you can take to become your best self.

I met Sheila when I spoke at one of Diversity Woman Media's conferences in 2019, before the world was changed by COVID-19. Sheila and I, drawn to each other over a shared interest in wellness and self-care, have built a strong connection. My interest in self-care stems from my practice as a chiropractor; Sheila's stems from a late but profound realization that her body and mind are her greatest assets.

When a cardiologist shook Sheila's world by telling her that while she was healthy at the time, she was at risk for future health problems because of her weight, Sheila knew it was time for a change. A doctor of education, Sheila suddenly became aware that while she had constantly pursued knowledge in leadership, parenthood, and other roles, she had never sought to educate herself about health and self-care.

Thus began a journey that led to a thirty-pound weight loss, a new model for self-care, a series of webinars during the pandemic called Wellness Wednesday, and this book. In her journey to educate herself, Sheila sought out experts in multiple areas of self-care and health. Her gleanings are included in the chapters you are about to read.

As I seek to educate my own clients, I want the information I share and the steps I suggest to be clear and understandable. None of us respond well to overwhelming prescriptions that uncomfortably turn our lives around. The changes that come with those prescriptions never last. We need to take bites we can chew and digest before we take another bite.

That's one reason I like Sheila's upending of the word *diet* to **D.I.E.T.**: **D** (drink), **I** (intake), **E** (exercise/activity), and **T** (think). It's chunked in ways I can understand and apply one step at a time. And the outcome is not just about pounds measured on a scale. It's about transforming how you look, feel, and perform.

So many women are drowning in the many responsibilities on their list: regular work, that extra project, kids, parents, boards, community, professional development, and more. Where will we get the energy? Only by investing in and rejoicing in self-care.

If you doubt that caring for yourself brings energy, read on to learn of the many expansions in business Sheila has accomplished in recent years, including the COVID-19 shutdown.

This book is not your usual diet, fitness, or health book. Sheila shares thoughtful insights and recommendations from experts as she guides us through her personal stories, recounting her successes and even some failures.

It hasn't been easy for her, and while we all have high expectations of ourselves, sometimes we just need to give ourselves a little kindness and gratitude. As I told Dr. Sheila in one of her Wellness Wednesday sessions: we all have A days, B days and C days. There's no reason to interpret a C day as a failure and give up. You just start over the next day.

How will you take small steps to do something good for your mental, physical, and spiritual self each day? Confucius says, "Life is really simple, but we insist on making it complicated." I say keep it simple and keep reading to learn how small changes can lead to transformation in your life.

Dr. Michelle Robin
September 2021

chapter one

My Story: What I Didn't Know Could Kill Me

My aha moment came when an abnormal EKG at an annual physical sent me to a cardiologist. When the cardiologist assured me that my heart was healthy, I breathed a sigh of relief—but that sigh was premature.

Rather than make a few notes in my electronic records and send me on my way, the doctor told me he was seriously concerned about my weight. Although I was healthy at that visit, I was, according to my BMI (body mass index), technically obese. If I continued carrying this excess weight around, I could—and most likely would—become unhealthy and contract the diseases for which I am at high risk because of my ethnicity and food choices. The big three I could expect were heart disease, diabetes, and hypertension.

As I listened to the doctor, somewhat stunned, I couldn't help but wonder how I had gotten to this point. I am an educated woman with a good income and access to healthy food choices. I had no reasonable excuse—except the one that virtually all women have: life had happened to me. A whole lot of ups, downs, successes, and challenges pulled my attention away from my most important and irreplaceable asset—my health.

In high school, I was one of the lucky ones. As a track star who won local and state championships, I held records in hurtles and performed as a cheerleader. I didn't need to worry about my weight in those days. Strong, fit, and confident, I enjoyed wearing clothes that flattered me. I always wanted to look and feel my best. In high school, it never occurred to me that this might be a challenge one day.

I also was a person with plans and reason to believe those plans would come true. I grew up in Winston Salem, North Carolina, the headquarters of R.J. Reynolds Tobacco Company. My father worked at the company, which had a policy of hiring the children of employees. My plan was to get my college degree, become a manager at the company, make plenty of money, marry, have children, and live the dream. Granted, this was a simplistic and self-centered plan, but it was mine—and it was firmly rooted in my mind. I'm the kind of person who always has a plan. I have a hard time with the saying, "The best laid plans of mice and men often go awry."

Fast-forward a few decades past high school: I was on a platform as host of a conference the company I founded, Diversity Woman Media, was holding. I had made it through a series of devastating career blows and was successful as an entrepreneur—a career to which my high school self would have said a firm *No, thank you*. I had a fan base and a diverse crowd of women who looked up to me and considered me an inspiration. I was also divorced, rebuilding my relationship with my only child, and thirty pounds heavier than my ideal weight based on my BMI.

I'd never lost the desire to look and feel my best, and yet my clothes didn't fit like they should. It seemed as if I had tried every diet and exercise program on the face of the earth, but there I was, still carrying the extra weight and its accompanying health and energy drain.

The conference was a high point in my professional and personal life. I couldn't have been more grateful for where I was professionally. I had found a higher purpose. Even so, after the adrenaline of the conference wore off, I looked in a mirror and wondered, *How did I let my body get to this point? What happened?*

The answer, once again, was simple: life had happened. With so many ups and downs between high school and the time of the conference, I had let certain things go. For many years, I focused on wading through the grief of a broken marriage, the challenges of parenting, the need to support myself after repeated layoffs, and the rigor of my doctoral program. Meanwhile, strategy after promising strategy to get my weight and level of fitness under control resulted in yet more failure. I wasn't in high school running track anymore. What could I expect?

It seemed time to accept that I had reached a weight heavily influenced by my age and that it was foolish to expect the number on my scale to substantially decrease. I set a new goal to maintain my current weight, to keep from gaining more. How many of us have reached this same point in life?

That whole line of logic shattered with the words of the cardiologist. I had to find a way to change. Thankfully, the cardiologist didn't leave me hanging. He suggested I buy two books: *Eat Move Sleep* by Tom Rath and *The South Beach Diet* by Arthur Agatston, MD.

I read those books and others, learning more about the needs of my body and making changes. Eventually, I found my personal path in a serendipitous way. A friend told me about an approach that worked for her. I tried it and found that the approach was the perfect fit for me too. Seemingly out of nowhere, I lost thirty pounds and was looking and feeling my best while succeeding in my career. The transformation in my body happened in less than six months, almost like magic. I lost the weight and gained energy and productivity in spades. Since then, I've continued to study and learn about the best ways to care for my body, this precious asset.

When I experienced a substantial increase in energy, feelings of well-being, and productivity, I immediately wanted to share what I was learning with other women. After all, the mission of Diversity Woman Media is to help smart, savvy women of all races, cultures, and backgrounds achieve their career and business goals. What goal-oriented professional woman isn't on a search for greater energy and productivity?

It's been three years since I lost the thirty pounds and experienced a personal and business transformation. I've been reading and researching about health and vitality the whole time. This, of course, does not make me an expert. I am neither a medical doctor nor a nutritionist. I'm a doctor of education with a story to tell. This book is my personal story, and I make no claim other than to own my story. I have no allegiance or affiliation with any program and none to recommend.

Redefining my understanding of diet and health has transformed the way I look, feel, and perform in my career. I believe the same can be true for you. You'll need to consult your own qualified medical and nutritional advisors to figure out what is right for you. You'll need to experiment and listen to your unique body. I simply have a story that I hope will inspire you to make your own health a priority so that you can reap rewards in how you feel and how you perform.

◇◇◇◇◇◇◇◇◇

I've learned that much of what I always thought was true about healthy practices around food and exercise is not true. The most fundamental and liberating thing I've learned is that a commitment to take care of my body isn't a commitment to spend my days in denial and self-sacrifice.

I've learned that our cultural understanding of diet is not only ugly, but also scientifically nonsensical. Proper caring for our bodies is so much more than counting calories and forcing down protein shakes. It can and should be an experience of joy and abundance.

I am eager to share my journey with you, but before I start, I want to share some foundational principles I've learned on along the way:

1. **There is no one-size-fits-all approach to health.** While I will describe what is working for me in this book, I will not necessarily recommend the same path for you. Your body is unique, and you must find its matching path to fitness and energy. By sharing my journey and including information from experts, I hope to inspire and inform you on your own journey toward optimal health. How you apply the information needs to be unique to you.

2. **Your thoughts are the most important ingredient for your success.** I say that my weight loss and energy transformation happened in less than six months, and that's true. It's also somewhat misleading.

In the years leading up to this transformation, especially during the three years just before it, I read or listened to countless books on leadership, overcoming adversity, goal setting, healthy living, and more. Changing and disciplining my thought life was foundational and fundamental to my success. The cardiologist supplied the urgency, but the groundwork was in place already. If you don't have your thought life in order, I recommend you focus there before you try any weight loss, productivity, or self-improvement program.

3. **Self-care and selfish are two different things.** Popular culture equates self-care with self-indulgence, including activities such as retail therapy, spa weekends, and cocktails with girlfriends. Nothing could be farther from the truth. Self-care is hard work that needs to become a discipline integrated into your daily life.

   In my life, self-care begins with a battle for joy and peace, regardless of circumstances. It means good food, rest, and movement, even when I'd rather binge on ice cream and on-demand TV. Self-care demands that we strive for self-love, self-value, and self-dignity in the noblest definitions of these terms. It means removing things and even people from our lives who obstruct us from these things. Once again, I can share my journey to self-care, but I can't prescribe what's right for you.

4. **Swap out Diets for D.I.E.T.** I've learned that diets don't work; they just waste time and make people feel bad about themselves. The very word *diet* connotes sacrifice, denial, and, perhaps especially, failure. This is the opposite of what we want from our lives. No wonder we cringe at the word.

Nearly all diets fall short because a) they are one-size-fits-all solutions, and b) they are artificial and therefore unsustainable. I finally found success when I stopped trying to diet and began thinking about providing my body with the nutrients and lifestyle it needs to flourish. I'm so excited to share what redefining D.I.E.T. has come to mean for me. For me, D.I.E.T. has come to stand for the following:

D = drink: Water is a vital nutrient we need to flourish. Many of us are chronically dehydrated. We aggravate the problem with alcohol, sugary drinks, and artificially flavored sodas. Often, when we feel hungry, we are actually thirsty.

I = intake: Everything we put into our systems contributes to our health or lack thereof. We need to take in and enjoy healthy foods such as vegetables and fruits and pay attention to what we inadvertently put into our bodies in various ways. For example, we may inadvertently take in aluminum from the way we cook our food and ward off body odor. We also need to be aware that we absorb much from our environment, including chemical toxins, criticism, and negativity.

E = exercise: When exercise feels like a burden and drudgery for us, we have a poor mindset or poor exercise fit—or both. I prefer to swap the words *activity* and *movement* for exercise. We all have activities we enjoy. If we think of all activity as exercise and build what we enjoy into our lives, we find pleasant anticipation where we once felt dread. Let's move—let's dance—to our own health!

T = think: Although thinking comes last in the acronym, it is by far the most important factor. Because our thoughts drive our reactions and behaviors, it's essential that we are aware of our thoughts and make choices about them. We can feed our brains the nutrients of positive, inspiring, motivating, and spiritual messages.

As we make our way through this book together, we will discuss each of the elements, *D, I, E,* and *T*. We will also explore how stress affects our bodies and how sleep, mindfulness, and supportive relationships help us heal and sustain health. We will discuss the importance of habit and routine in sustaining health and look at examples of how others have built positive routines into their health regimens. In the context of this information and my stories, you'll have the opportunity to examine your own practices and routines and generate a plan for redefining your own D.I.E.T.

◇◇◇◇◇◇◇◇

I don't know what your journey toward looking and feeling your best has been so far. If you are like most women, however, that journey hasn't been easy. You've had many things in life to distract you, both personally and professionally. You've been fed false information about diet and exercise, including the idea that the foods that are best for you taste bad, and that ice cream straight from the carton is the ultimate comfort food.

You've repeatedly received the message that self-care is self-indulgence, and that you should feel guilty when you care for yourself. After all, if you are a woman, you are a caregiver and need to spend your energy on others.

If you are a leader in the workplace, you've been led to believe that long hours and sacrifice are in your job description. If you want to succeed, chances are you've been told that you must work harder than your male peers.

All this negativity ends now. If you get nothing else from this book, get this: you are worth it. Good health is a state of abundance and joy. You deserve to care for your body, mind, and spirit, and you have a responsibility to do so.

You are the one charged with investing in your own life. This isn't selfishness; it's your right. What's more, when you care for yourself on a daily basis, you'll find that you have more energy and higher productivity to perform your many responsibilities. You'll be stronger and better able to deal with adversity. What is most important is that you'll have more joy and the energy to share that joy with all those who touch your life.

A new path is calling you, and it is unique to you. I'm going to share some things I have tried, read, been coached on, and applied with good results. These are manageable behaviors I plan to continue for the rest of my life—ones that are available to you as well. Most important, I encourage you to use my experience as a springboard to find what is right for you. I feel confident that whatever that right path is for you, it will have the redefined D.I.E.T. as an underlying foundation. Are you ready to transform how you look, feel, and perform in your career? Let's get started.

chapter two

Refreshing News: What Diet Is NOT

Chances are that like me, you have a lifelong, unhappy relationship with the word *diet*. The very thought of the word used to fill me with anxiety and dread. It's an ugly word, full of accusation and judgment.

If I needed to diet, it was because I was fat. If I was *fat*, it was because I had *failed* to live up to the standard set for me by outside sources. Subconsciously or consciously, I measured myself against that standard my entire adult life.

I never questioned who set the standard—at least as it related to me. I knew that our culture's media messages were skewed and based on corporate greed. I also knew that the example of the ideal female body, as defined by that media, was impossible for nearly all women to attain.

Even so, I had an internal image of how I should look—how I should present myself to the world. That image included a list of not-more-than qualities—not more than size twelve, not more than a certain hip size, waist size, etc.

As a professional woman, I considered this image as much a matter of executive presence as health. Reflecting back, I realize that *looking* healthy took precedence over *being* healthy. I was too busy as a wife, mom, and professional to focus on being healthy. There would always be time for that—later.

Like many women, I took my health for granted, rather than realizing that my health was an asset that either enhanced or limited my productivity, based on the quality of fuel, sleep, and other factors I gave it. I just never saw the connection. I took more care in putting the correct fuel and maintenance into my car than I did into my body.

I dieted to look good and hated the experience. Dieting was in the must-do category—because I wasn't good enough. It was a punishment for being undisciplined and out of shape. To me, diet meant that I could neither eat nor enjoy food. It meant being restricted or deprived of foods, especially the ones that I loved. It meant filling my stomach with food that had no flavor. It meant miniature portions and always hungry feeling. It also meant no desserts, no pizza, no cake.

Fortunately, beginning with the resources my cardiologist recommended, I began to shift my understanding of some words, including diet, nutrition, and health.

With that doctor's visit, my focus on achieving and maintaining a healthy body shifted from something I would like to do to something I must do—at least if I wanted to continue with my active lifestyle. If I contracted the heart disease, diabetes, or hypertension the doctor warned me of, my life would be seriously limited. If I wanted to achieve my definition of personal and professional success and enjoyment, I needed to change my priorities. I needed to engage in self-care, something most women are conditioned to put last on the priority list.

My first step was to begin educating myself. As my doctor had suggested, I read *The South Beach Diet* by Arthur Agatston, MD. I quickly fell in love with this book because, to my surprise, it was not about restriction or sacrifice. I found myself reading about the foods I *could* eat on my journey to health.

Scanning the list of recommended foods, I realized that I had become conditioned to choose foods that society told me were tasty, indulgent, celebratory, or—especially alluring for my hectic lifestyle—fast. In fact, I knew that most of the foods on the *South Beach* list were delicious as well as nutritious. I had just been ignoring them.

In my family, fried foods, pastas, and sugary desserts were part of every celebration, so naturally I associated them with good living. When eating out, I chose the high-fat, salty, and sugary foods that society told me were desirable. When on my own, I chose snacks and foods I could quickly consume, allowing me to get back to my important tasks. As a result, my palate craved these foods, and the habits I had formed, as well as the taste of cheese and salty chips, kept me coming back for more.

Meanwhile, I was ignoring a host of foods that taste better and deliver superior fuel to my body. I began adding foods from the *South Beach* list into my eating patterns and noticing how my palate reacted. In fact, I began tasting rather than gulping foods for the first time in a long while. I savored blueberries, apples, seafood, lean proteins, oatmeal, avocados, green leafy vegetables, zucchini, carrots, and many more foods. Because there are no portion limits on these foods, I could eat as much as I wanted. Smaller amounts of healthy fats—such as olive oil and a variety of nuts—are recommended, and the flavors and satiation of these foods go a long way.

Some of the items on the "ideal foods" list turned out to be good for me, but I didn't like them. For example, I just don't like juices or cottage cheese. That's okay because there are plenty of foods on the list I do like.

In this process, I became an observer of my own body, not just in how specific foods taste to me but in how those foods make me feel. I learned that refined carbohydrates, such as white pasta and crackers, leave me feeling sluggish. Sugar and highly processed foods leave me feeling low and rather down soon after eating them.

As I began adding new, nutritious foods to my diet, my attention was drawn away from those foods that aren't as good for me. These foods were, in a sense, crowded out of my diet. And my palate changed to crave the new foods. Planning for and preparing these foods does take time, but I found the payoff is well worth it. I began to see a decrease in my weight and an increase in my energy level. When eating, I was tasting my food and genuinely enjoying it.

Diet Is a Noun—Not a Verb

I educated myself about healthy living through books, articles, podcasts, conversations, and more. I don't want to pretend I became an expert in health and nutrition, but my way of thinking was transformed. I want to share that shift in perspective with you.

One of the biggest changes came in the way I understood the word *diet*. I realized that diet is not something I am either "on" or "off." Diet is what I eat or drink, no matter how much, how often, or the number of calories. It is all my diet. My diet is everything that I eat, drink, and consume daily. For a comparison, if we were learning about the energy sources of a particular bird, we would list the insects, seeds, and water that bird consumes. This would describe the bird's diet—it's not that the bird is on a diet.

Everyone has a diet, whether the person is paying attention to it or not. You may choose a diet that consists of mostly vegetables or a diet that consists mostly of milkshakes—or any combination thereof. Whatever your choices, you have a diet.

Nutrition is different from diet. Nutrition refers to the quality of the food itself. Highly nutritious foods support your body's goal of functioning at an optimal level. The best diet, I've learned, is one that is good for all parts of your body—from your brain to your toes, not just your waistline.

Plenty of diet programs prescribe restrictions (sometimes weird ones) and meal plans to help you lose weight. These choices aren't necessarily good for your health. In fact, you can be at a reasonable weight and not be healthy—lacking optimal energy, productivity, and resistance to disease.

I encourage you to begin improving your diet by thinking more about what your body *needs* rather than how much you weigh. This is especially important for women because we are taught to care for others while devaluing our own needs.

Emily and Amelia Nagoski, twin sisters and the authors of *Burnout: The Secret to Unlocking the Stress Cycle*, point out a great divide in how women think about the bodies of their babies versus their own bodies. We coo at our infant girls, celebrating their chubby cheeks, tummies, and thighs. As adults, if chubby can describe any part of our own bodies, even our toes, we judge ourselves as ugly. We shame ourselves. When does the shift from body love to body hate happen?

The Nagoski sisters suggest an exercise that may help you to listen to your body, to genuinely love it and notice what it needs. Rather than evaluate and judge your body by how it looks, turn to your inner girl and ask how she feels. Ask if she is tired, hungry, or thirsty. Consider giving the girl inside you this message from the authors:

> *Your body needs to breathe and to sleep. She needs food. She needs love. She dies without them. And there is nothing she has to do, no shape or size she has to be, before she "deserves" food and love and sleep. It's not her fault if she's sick or injured. She's still the astonishing creature she was on the day she was born, a source of joy for those who care about her. She is yours. She's you.*

If you find it awkward to think of lovingly caring for your body rather than judging or punishing yourself, it's time to change your perspective. Your needs are as important as the needs of those around you. Honor yourself and your body's needs. Give your body good nutrition, the focus of this chapter. Of course, there are more elements to health than eating well, and we'll talk about some of these things in later chapters.

You can find differing opinions about the most important foods to include or and exclude from your chosen diet, but most experts recommend a balanced mix to ensure that your body gets the nutrients it needs to function optimally. To get the proper nutrition, you should consume most of your daily calories in fresh vegetables, fresh fruits, whole grains, beans, legumes, nuts, and lean proteins.

By most accounts, ideal food choices include romaine lettuce, flaxseed, sweet potatoes, raw nuts, seeds, salmon, berries, citrus fruit, oatmeal, quinoa, olive oil, spinach, avocado, Greek yogurt, and dark chocolate. When it comes to good nutrition, these foods give you a great bang for your buck. Fortunately, herbs and spices, which add flavor, are nutritious as well. Superstars include cinnamon, rosemary, saffron, ginger, oregano, and turmeric.

One evidence-based way to celebrate food and increase the nutrition in your diet—without making things complicated—is to eat and enjoy colors of the rainbow. The differing natural colors in fresh vegetables and fruits have specific healing properties.

Taken directly from a post by the Mayo Clinic, here is what eating the rainbow of colors can do for you:

- Red fruits and vegetables may reduce the risk of osteoporosis and diabetes, along with inhibiting the formation of cholesterol in blood.
- Orange and yellow fruits and vegetables contain beta carotene, known for playing a vital role in maintaining healthy eyesight and night vision.
- Green fruits and vegetables contain antioxidants that are shown to protect the retina in the eye and preserve vision and prevent blindness.
- White, tan, and brown fruits and vegetables help maintain heart health and lower the risk of certain cancers.
- Blue and purple fruits and vegetables have anti-inflammatory properties and can reduce cholesterol levels, help prevent atherosclerosis, support blood flow, and help fight the onset of glaucoma.

All these are foods you *can* eat, as much as your heart desires. I hope that one of the things you take from this book is that educating yourself about a healthy diet is more about learning what you *can* eat and enjoy than depriving yourself of foods that you already know aren't good for you.

I happened to learn about foods I can eat with joy and abandon through the South Beach Diet, but another source might work better for you. You might investigate the Mediterranean diet or the anti-inflammatory diet. A friend of mine found her list of nutritious foods from the *Anticancer Book* by David Servan-Schreiber. Consider sources that list and provide recipes for superfoods and the best foods for a healthy gut. While the lists you find may be shorter or longer, experts agree on the top contenders. And dark chocolate is now an established superfood!

Once again, I'm not trying to set myself up as an expert in anything except my own story. I encourage you to do your own research.

As you know, experts also agree on the top contenders of foods that hurt rather than help your body. You don't need me to tell you that processed foods, high fat entrees, and soft drinks are not good for you. Processed foods are loaded with sugar, stripped of fiber, and chemically altered to be addictive. They are filled with artificial chemicals, unhealthy fats, and sodium. These foods cause spikes in insulin that can lead to many problems, including poor sleep, while filling your stomach with empty calories rather than nutrition. Still, we love these foods. We've been conditioned to equate certain foods with love and "the good life" since before we can remember.

Making a list of such foods and labeling them *never* is unwise and unrealistic. The best diet is one that is flexible and sustainable for you over the long haul. One reason people lose and gain weight in a yo-yo fashion is because they experience diet as a verb, a way they restrict themselves until they get their weight under control. Once they hit the target weight, the restrictions are hard to maintain.

Here's a question for you: What would happen if instead of thinking of diet as a dreaded and restrictive thing you do to lose weight (and thinking of yourself as a loser), you began a quest to love your body with foods that support and heal it? What if you took the idea that "food is love" and defined that in whole different way?

If you can make this mental shift, losing weight is only one of the benefits you'll enjoy. In my own journey, I was surprised to discover that maintaining a healthy weight isn't the biggest benefit from eating well. It's nice, but it's just a side benefit compared to the increase in energy, positive moods, and productivity. I feel good, and I look good, but more important, I can do good—for myself and others. I can contribute more than I ever have before.

A Healthy Diet Isn't All or Nothing

Switching to a healthy and nutritious diet doesn't have to be an all or nothing proposition. You don't have to be perfect, you don't have to completely eliminate foods you enjoy, and you don't have to change everything all at once—that usually only leads to cheating or giving up on your new eating plan.

An effective way to make changes in any area of life is to make a few small changes at a time. Keeping your goals modest can help you achieve more in the long term without feeling deprived or overwhelmed by a major overhaul. Think of planning a healthy diet as a series of small, manageable steps—like adding a salad to your diet once a day. As your small changes become habit, you can continue to add more healthy choices.

To set yourself up for success, try to keep things simple. Although a complete understanding of good nutrition and optimal body functioning is complicated, eating a healthier diet doesn't have to be. Begin by thinking of your diet in terms of color, variety, and freshness. Increase your intake of fresh ingredients, especially fresh vegetables, to crowd out packaged and processed foods.

I have found that following the 80/20 rule allows me to be realistic and enjoy life while maintaining a healthy lifestyle. If I eat foods that support and heal my body 80 percent of the time, I feel comfortable enjoying almost anything I want to eat 20 percent of the time. For me, this means popcorn for my go-to snack and fried chicken and perhaps birthday cake at family celebrations. If you want to be more aggressive, Michelle Robin, DC, who has been a great resource for this book, recommends you follow an 85/15 rule. (You'll learn more about Dr. Robin and her tips as the book unfolds.)

As I enjoy any food, I act as a detective, always noticing how my body feels after it takes in different foods. I find that certain foods make me feel sluggish, down, and/or bloated. When I listen, my body tells me what is good for it and what's not. And I've learned that it is silly to feel bad for hours for the pleasure of a few bites of food, especially when there are so many foods that are both energizing and delicious.

The strategies to add greater nutrition to your diet are endless. Here are some I've come across in my reading:

- Add one vegetable to each meal.
- Replace one serving of a processed food with a serving of a vegetable or fruit.

- Divide your plate for health. Use one third of the plate for a protein and two thirds of the plate for plant-based foods.
- Experiment with healthy whole grains to see which ones you like. Try wild rice, kasha, quinoa, bulgur, barley, and whole wheat couscous.
- Experiment with plant-based milks to see which ones appeal to you. Try almond milk, coconut milk, soy milk, etc. Experiment with plant-based butters as well.
- Serve fresh fruit over Greek yogurt in place of a sugary desert.
- Try water flavored with fresh fruit or mint in place of a soda or diet soda.
- For breakfast, try Greek yogurt topped with berries and nuts in place of prepared fruited yogurt. Sweeten with honey or agave if needed. Add some ground flax seed, and you have a powerhouse of nutrients.
- Keep a bottle or glass of water on your desk and sip often.
- Drink a glass of water to hydrate yourself first thing in the morning.
- At the office, take a walking break around the office instead of a trip to the vending machine.
- Dedicate a few hours on the weekend to prepare healthy meals and snacks you can eat throughout the week.

One important strategy involves shifting your beliefs about the food ingredients that make a good party, celebration, or dinner with friends. We assume—often wrongly—that others equate a good time with high-fat entrees, sweet deserts, and copious amounts of alcohol. Add or contribute some healthy options to your next gathering. Here some examples:

- Offer flavored water along with other drink options.
- Include hummus and fresh vegetables with your appetizers.
- Bring a flavorful fresh salad to your next potluck. Make a homemade salad dressing, flavored with herbs in place of the bottled dressing, which contains sugar and preservatives.
- Serve grilled or roasted vegetables to bring out a naturally sweet flavor.
- Serve grilled or roasted fruit sprinkled with nuts as a dessert option.

Diet, used as a verb, will always be an ugly word. I've dropped it from my vocabulary, and so can you. This book is about redefining your D.I.E.T., as a noun, in ways that allow you to effectively love and care for yourself so that you can live the life you want, with energy, vitality, and productivity.

In this chapter about what diet is not, we have begun talking about things related to *D* for drink and *I* for intake. There's more to come about both in chapters 6 and 7. A key point here is that the best diet (noun) is one that is good for your entire body, from your brain to your toes, and is sustainable for the long haul.

Although this kind of diet, the particulars of which will be unique to you, is delicious and satisfying, forces will constantly push you to derail it. The media, and even well-meaning family and friends, will urge you to eat foods and drinks that are lacking in nutrition and can make you feel lousy. Many of these foods introduce toxins into your body. The media will push the foods to get your money, and your friends will push them to include you in their perception of celebration and the good life.

Fortunately, the more you eat nutritious food, the more your body will crave it. That's the beginning of a positive cycle. Even so, you'll need more. One critical ingredient is a healthy mindset, the topic of the next chapter.

Five Reasons to Make Small Changes
By Michelle Robin, DC

Whether I work with clients one on one, speak to small groups, or address huge auditoriums, my approach is the same—small changes create big shifts.

There is a caveat to that. If you are in an acute health crisis, you may need to take a more dramatic approach to get your body out of crisis mode. Only you and your healthcare practitioner can know that. However, for the rest of us, it is good to deepen and broaden our knowledge about health and wellness and then take it one step at a time. Here are five reasons to do just that:

1. **You can really see/feel the impact.** If you suddenly change a lot of things in your behavior, eating habits, sleeping, etc., all at once you won't really know how each action is making you feel. I speak about "Body Talk." If you make small changes, you can really listen to your body and feel how that particular change is making a difference (or not) and adjust accordingly—more, less, or differently.

2. **You can avoid feeling overwhelmed, physically or emotionally.** When you pile on the changes, especially when they're significantly different from the lifestyle you had been living, you can feel overwhelmed. Making dramatic changes all at once can create a lot of stress in your mental space and in your body. Why put yourself through that if you don't have to? Small changes, one at a time, give you the ease of focus.

3. **You can handle imperfections better.** If you choose to make small changes, you are less likely to fall into an all or nothing mindset if you slip up one day. You know what I'm talking about: when you say yes to the birthday cake in the office Friday afternoon—even though you're trying to cut out sugar—and later that night you say, *Forget it.* I might as well have Chinese takeout and cheesecake tonight.

4. **You can focus on creating a new healthy habit.** Research tells us that it takes a minimum of twenty-one days to create a new habit (ninety days to really ingrain it). If you're serious about making changes in your health and well-being, healthier actions need to be long-term habits, not

one-and-done quick fixes. If you take on one small change at a time, it will be easier to give that change the attention and intention it deserves to become a new healthy habit.

5. **You will feel the compound effect of success.** When you succeed, you naturally feel the drive to create more success. Every single day you are successful gives you the zing of pride and self-satisfaction, not to mention improving your health and feeling better. The good feelings motivate you to keep it up. When you've built up a bank of success, you're more capable of handling a small debit (slip in a healthy habit) if you don't quite make it happen on a particular day. The compound effect of success spurs you to take on new small changes when you're ready and feel more confident in your ability to make them stick.

Small changes are the best approach to creating healthy habits to improve your well-being. Now, how can you apply this to your wellness journey? What small change will you focus on first?

Adapted from https://www.drmichellerobin.com/5-reasons-make-small-changes/

chapter three

Essential Foundation: Mindset

During my pregnancy with my one beautiful child, I gained a lot of weight. Once Leah was born, I was deeply in love with my girl—and deeply *dis*satisfied with my weight. While I wish I had simply enjoyed my baby, my new role as a mom, and marveled at the miracle of how a woman's body gives and recovers from making a new life, I expended energy stressing about many things and judging my body.

I wanted to reach my ideal weight, in part because I wanted to be appealing to my husband. Of course, I also had the mental image of how a successful professional woman should look: trim, toned, and energetic. I realize now that taking care of my body to please a person or an external standard is an unhealthy driver. While nothing is wrong with the natural desire to be sexually pleasing, our relationship with our bodies should be about us, about our love and care for ourselves and this most precious asset we have.

Following Leah's birth, I was anything but energetic. When it came to making the adjustments needed to parent a newborn, I wasn't gifted with a roll-with-the-punches personality. I was stressed out and exhausted. Adding to my stress was a struggle many women go through: I was wrestling with conflicting feelings about returning to full-time work. Although I loved my corporate job at DuPont at that time, as a first-time mom my love and attachment to Leah had me dreading my return to work. I had fallen in love with my daughter and struggled with the thought of not being with her 24/7. I even tried to persuade my husband that it would be best for our family if I quit.

The emotion connected to this internal conflict, the heavy responsibilities at work, concerns about my parenting skills, worries about childcare during work hours, lack of sleep, keeping up a household, and trying to please my husband, boss, and family members kept me in a continual state of stress. While your particulars might be different, chances are you know what I'm talking about.

If a friend had come to me in the state of stress I was in at the time, I would have advised that friend to be kind and gentle with herself. I would have encouraged her to have realistic expectations during this season of adjustment—and care for herself while she was caring for others. I would have told this friend that her spirit as well as her body needed time to recover and adjust and reminded her that there was no rush to find the highest and most productive level of a new normal. I would have advised my friend to talk with her husband about her feelings and his needs (not his expectations) and work as partners to make the best life for their fledgling family of three.

Not having the wisdom to be a good friend to myself, I joined Weight Watchers and lost eight pounds. Losing that weight was nice although it didn't get me near my ideal goal—and I gained the weight back. Does this mean Weight Watchers is a bad program? No.

The problem was with my drivers. The *why* I had for pursuing weight loss was not strong enough because it didn't come from pleasing or caring for myself. I was also approaching Weight Watchers with a short-term perspective, looking for a short-term fix. I got exactly that—a loss of eight pounds for a short duration.

This strategy failed to work for me over the long term for multiple reasons, all having to do with misdirected attention, wrong assumptions, and/or a misguided mindset.

- I considered my well-being a low priority, something that might get attention when others' needs and my various responsibilities were met. I accepted the perspective that it was okay—and even expected—that working women, especially moms, would be continually overworked, stressed, and exhausted.
- I thought of my weight as an independent category—separate from other aspects of my personhood. I thought of myself as a healthy person who happened to be overweight. My body was a tool that required no special fuel or maintenance, expect perhaps a yearly physical, where I would be told I needed to lose weight.
- I ignored some proven health realities, including the fact that many diseases, including heart disease and diabetes, play a long and insidious game, with excess weight *over time* being a significant risk factor.
- Without thinking much about it, I expected my energy and productivity to function at a consistently high level over time, whether I took care of myself or not.
- Rather than listening to my body when it sent signals that I was sleep deprived, sad, or stressed, I simply pushed harder, believing I could ignore my body's signals without consequences.
- Rather than extending compassion to myself, I berated myself for lack of discipline and willpower.

Yikes! When I look at this list of misdirected attention, wrong assumptions, and my misguided mindset, I cringe. You don't need special credentials to quickly see that when it came to my personal well-being, I was living an unexamined life. I was on autopilot, which stemmed from messages I had absorbed from the culture around me. I definitely wasn't using my brain.

Today, I think of my body as my most precious personal and business asset. Investing time, attention, and care for my body is as high a priority for me as investing in my family and my business.

I've had a profound shift in mindset. How did this shift occur?

Brian Keane, author of *The Fitness Mindset: Eat for Energy, Train for Tension, Manage Your Mindset, Reap the Results*, would say I found a new *why* to pay attention to my health.

When the cardiologist explained to me that failing to lose the excess weight would literally be choosing to shave years off my life, everything inside me shifted. While I knew and accepted that we are all going to die someday, I didn't want to be responsible for shortening my own time on earth. I still don't.

Keane points out that it's easy to find surface reasons to get fit, as I did throughout my adult life. These include the desire to look better, feel better, and be attractive to the opposite sex. Surface reasons are okay to get us started, but they don't have the power to sustain us through plateaus and days when we just don't feel up to the task.

To continually practice the behaviors that lead to good health, we need a powerful *why*. If we don't have one, chances are our goals for weight and fitness will end up like most New Year's resolutions. We will start out with a big commitment and keep it up for a few weeks or months. Then life will get in the way, and we'll lose momentum. Before long, everything will be back to where it's always been.

When this cycle repeats itself, we judge ourselves for our lack of willpower and add yet another layer of negativity around the task of getting fit and staying fit. Whatever weight we lost in the effort, we gain back—and then some.

According to Keane, a powerful *why* will drive the how. In my story, the *why* came from my visit with the cardiologist. Shortly thereafter, a friend told me about the success she was having with a specific program, and I made an investment to try that program myself.

When I had immediate results with the program, I was energized to keep going. Eventually, I shifted from that original program to intermittent fasting, which has been a sustainable strategy for me. More about this later.

I think I might have had good results with any number of programs at the outset—because the compelling *why* had so altered my mindset. I've come to believe the words I first heard from Shanequa Fleming, EdD, CEO of

Culture Accelerators and strategic advisor to executives and senior leadership teams: mindset comes before skill set. Even with the right mindset, losing and keeping my pounds off took time and patience. Without that right mindset, I believe it would be impossible for me, at least without feeling deprived and miserable.

Now, even on the days I don't feel like eating right or keeping to my fitness practices, I remember the compelling *why* I choose these things. The food I eat to stay healthy is more important to me than indulging any cravings I have. I am not perfect, but I do seek to be joyful.

As I mentioned earlier, I stick with healthy eating 80 percent of the time and eat whatever I want the other 20 percent. This allows me room to regularly savor my favorite snack of cheese popcorn. It also allows me to approach a family gathering or celebration with the freedom to enjoy fried chicken and an occasional slice of birthday cake. This works for me; I enjoy life and maintain a healthy weight. And remember, 80 percent of the time I'm celebrating and enjoying the many foods that are both delicious and full of nutrition.

As soon as I found my compelling *why* to prioritize my health, I began to educate myself on the topic. Along the way, I've discovered some great sources of knowledge and inspiration. Among these is Dr. Michelle Robin, prolific author, and founder of Small Changes Big Shifts, a website packed with resources on whole-person well-being. Dr. Robin helped me understand a foundational truth: As a leader, mother, partner, and friend, I cannot be fully present if something is amiss in my body, mind, or spirit. I'm a complete package.

I love the way Dr. Robin phrased it in an interview with me:

> *I think about Jesus and Mother Teresa walking down the streets and people becoming healed just by their vibration. They didn't have to say a word. They just walked by, and people had hope and healing.*
>
> *That's how we're designed to be. We're designed to bring the light into rooms, but when we don't feel good, if we have a bellyache, a headache,*

anxiety, or depression, we can't be good leaders. We just can't show up at 100 percent.

I believe that we each deserve to live a full life. That alone is a compelling reason to take care of ourselves. I've also come to understand that self-care, a topic we'll examine in detail in the next chapter, is as important as anything else I do. In fact, the things I do to keep my body, mind, and spirit healthy enable me to fully contribute to the world. Self-care is foundational to my productivity as a business owner, my effectiveness as a leader, my nurturing as a mother, and my support as a friend. If I were still married, it would be foundational to partnering with my spouse.

The mindset I'm describing here is a far cry from the one I unthinkingly embraced after I gave birth to my daughter more than twenty years ago. Since then, I've examined and revised my assumptions and what I pay attention to. My mindset now includes the following beliefs:

- Under no circumstances is it a badge of honor to be overworked, stressed, and exhausted. Because my well-being is as important as everyone else's, I behave responsibly when I take care of my body, mind, and spirit.
- My weight is but one indication of my body's health. Weight is integral to my overall health and well-being. Other factors, including healthy sleep habits and regular spiritual practices, are integral as well.
- Short-term perspectives don't work when it comes to my health and well-being. To be my best self and prevent disease, I need to discover and commit to healthy practices I can sustain over time.
- Self-care is a leadership, relational, and parental best practice. To achieve my highest levels of productivity in *any* area, I must consistently care for myself.
- I need to listen to my body as a source of wisdom. When my body sends signals that it is sleep deprived, sad, or stressed, I must adjust accordingly or suffer the consequences.
- I am worthy of the same compassion I extend to my friends.

- A less-than-successful day is not a failure or reason to quit my journey toward well-being. My goal in this book is to share my transformational story in the hopes that it inspires you to examine your life in ways that lead you to greater well-being and productivity. As you know, I've redefined diet to D.I.E.T. (drink, intake, exercise, and thoughts).

You can see that the final letter, *T*, points to the importance of our thoughts. In fact, success in achieving well-being ends and begins with our thoughts. That's *why* this chapter comes early in the book.

In my interview with Dr. Robin, I shared my thoughts on D.I.E.T. After a pause, she responded, "You know, Sheila, without the *T*, all you have is DIE. That's how important our thoughts are."

Dr. Robin also taught me that I can think of any bad day as over with the close of the day. The next day is a fresh start.

Have you examined your thoughts about well-being and self-care lately?

What's Your Mindset?

Researcher Carol Dweck, PhD, was initially intrigued by how different children responded to failure to complete a puzzle set before them. Dr. Dweck noticed that some children actually embraced a difficult challenge or failure as an opportunity to learn. Sparked by that observation, Dr. Dweck spent thirty years researching people's beliefs about failure.

Dr. Dweck published a groundbreaking book called *Mindset: The New Psychology of Success*, which changed the way experts talk about mental constructs regarding learning and failure. We tend to learn one of two mindsets from our parents, teachers, and other authority figures. The two options are *fixed mindset* and *growth mindset*.

People with a fixed mindset believe, consciously or unconsciously, that the intelligence, abilities, and talents they have were present at birth. In other words, these qualities are fixed and can't be changed. This mindset creates a need to project competence and strength while hiding any weaknesses. Nobody wants to be perceived as inferior. If you diagnose yourself with imposter syndrome (you experience yourself at some level as a fraud who fears she will be found out), chances are you have a fixed mindset.

Those children Dr. Dweck observed who embraced failure as a learning opportunity obviously didn't have a fixed mindset. These children had a growth mindset, which is based on the belief that intelligence, abilities, and talents can be cultivated through effort, strategy, and help from others. When people with a growth mindset don't feel they measure up to a task or challenge, they seek to get better. They may choose to do research, build a skill, ask an expert, or experiment with options. Generally speaking, they don't feel the need to hide the fact they have room for improvement.

When it comes to well-being, would you describe your mindset as fixed or growth-oriented? Do you look at your weight or other biomedical markers and think there's nothing you can do about them? Do you pretend to practice mindfulness and other wellness practices while thinking you are a hopeless case? If so, you might want to consider the overall mindset you bring to life.

People with a growth mindset believe that the abilities they are born with are simply a starting point. From this perspective, difficulties—and even failure—don't need to be a source of embarrassment. Education can help you see things from new perspectives, and experience is a great teacher.

If you've repeatedly failed at diets, exercise plans, meditation techniques, and spiritual practices, don't let yourself believe you are a failure or forever stuck. Take one small step in the right direction and see what happens. If the step you try doesn't work, try a different step. Most important, don't isolate in your struggle. To succeed, we need each other. Your friend or colleague may have the exact insight that you need to grow.

Learn more in Carol S. Dweck, PhD. *Mindset: The New Psychology of Success*, Ballantine Books, 2007.

chapter four

Creating a Space for Success: Self-care

It was some time after my divorce before I was able to settle down and look at how my own shortcomings and choices had contributed to the unraveling of my marriage.

You might look at me now—at my business and multiple commitments—and wonder if I had too many irons in the fire to give my marriage, daughter, and home the attention each deserved. You might see me speaking at a conference and guess that the problem might be my high ambitions or a need to be front and center. In fact, the reality was quite a different thing.

My desire to advance my career and make good money wasn't about me seeking recognition or accolades for myself. I envisioned a good job as a path to contribute financially to the household, and this, I assumed, would make my husband happy.

I entered marriage with an unexamined belief that if I kept my husband, daughter, boss, and extended community happy, I would, by extension, be happy. Actually, I believed that if everyone else was happy, I'd be over the moon.

Naturally, I set out to keep others happy. This was my mission all day, every day. My being happy was little more than an afterthought, an expected outcome of keeping everyone else happy. It's sad that I never thought further than that.

It did not occur to me to define what happiness for myself would look like, let alone pursue such a thing. I've come to realize that this omission, in addition to devaluing myself, contributed to the conditions for an unworkable marriage.

I am accountable for failing to put my own needs into the family equation. I didn't even realize I had needs, passions, and a purpose of my own. These things were buried so deep within me that I wouldn't have recognized them if they jumped out at me. Even if I had recognized my needs, I would have judged it selfish to pursue them in the face of so many other pressing responsibilities. Perhaps you share this perspective, at least to some degree. Perhaps the idea of putting yourself first seems selfish and self-centered to you—but there's something to be said for it.

Many, if not most, women are raised with the idea that selflessness is somewhere next to godliness, especially for working moms. I finally realized how foolish this is when I read an article that used the oxygen mask on an airplane as an example.

On every single flight, the flight attendant describes a practice that can make the difference between life and death. "In case of emergency, put your own mask on first. Only then will you be able to help those around you, including your children, other family members, and business associates."

This analogy isn't new, and I'm sure I had heard it before, but the truth behind it hadn't registered. On this particular day, the analogy blew me away. I could see that taking care of myself was different from making life all about me. Rather than being selfish, it was being wise. If I had done the necessary things to make myself healthy and productive mentally, physically, and spiritually, I would have been so much better at taking care of all the other things on my plate.

Emma J. Bell, founder of The Global Resilience Project and author of *9 Secrets to Thriving*, shares an analogy that makes the same point. Bell uncovered the analogy in an interview with Helen, a woman who survived a terrorist attack that killed her husband and thirteen-year-old daughter.

Helen managed to rebound and thrive even after this horrific experience. Talking about self-care, Helen asked Bell to think about her mobile phone. She said, "You wouldn't not charge your phone and expect it to work, would you? So don't expect 'you' to work if you don't take care of yourself. You will drain all your energy and become emotionally and mentally exhausted."

Defining Self-care

During much of my working and parenting years, my idea of self-care had more to do with my "shoulds" regarding my body than with whole-person self-care. I knew I was letting some things go, but those things weren't important to me. For example, I neither ate well nor exercised, although I knew I should do both. If I was in a rush, I would eat anything I could stuff into my mouth on the fly. I might skip lunch to keep working and then feel as if I were starving on the way home. I'd stop for fast food to fortify myself to cook dinner for my husband and daughter. On days my daughter needed a ride to an afterschool event, I picked up fast food, believing I didn't have time to cook.

I didn't exercise and, at some level, I considered this a badge of honor. I mean, how could I exercise? Anyone could see all the responsibilities on my plate. What full-time working mom of a young child has time to exercise?

In addition to my shoulds, I had a lot of "whens." I had a mantra that began, "When I get past this . . ." I'd say to myself, "*When I get past these early years and my daughter is in kindergarten, I'll . . .*" or, "*When we finish building this house . . .*"

There was always something that had to happen first. Meanwhile, when I felt overwhelmed, stressed, or sorry for myself, I'd indulge in my favorite high-calorie, nutritionally deficient foods. The pounds piled on, and I felt continually sluggish. I soldiered on because that's what good caregivers and professional women do.

It turned out that my daughter had graduated from college before I changed my lifestyle enough that I could lose a pound and not gain it right back. By then, however, I was starting to understand that while self-care includes weight management and exercise, it is bigger than those things. That was in 2018. I still had a long way to go.

My 2020 conversation with Shanequa Fleming, EdD, covered many topics including leadership, productivity, and self-care. I was particularly struck when Dr. Fleming said, "Leadership is about connection. To support and encourage those whom we lead, we must create a space, whether it be physical or virtual, where people can flourish and be genuinely free to show up in their individual and respective zones of genius."

What a beautiful definition of leadership. What a beautiful definition of flourishing.

Implicit in Dr. Fleming's definition of leadership is a definition of self-care. Each of us has the right and responsibility to seek out what we need to flourish, even as we negotiate our relationships and responsibilities. We need to identify and secure for ourselves that which is necessary to fully show up in our own personal and professional zone of genius. This is self-care.

Where did I get the idea that self-care was limited to the disciplines of eating well and exercising? Boy, did I have a lot to learn. Certainly, self-care involves the body. Each of us, however, is much more than a body. We are minds, spirits, passions, and purpose too.

I asked Nancy O'Reilly, PsyD, founder of Women Connect4Good, to talk to me about self-care. She said, "Self-care comes down to worth, self-worth. It's about what you deserve."

Zeroing in on what we, as leaders, need to hear, Dr. O'Reilly continued, "You want everyone you work with to totally show up, and a person can't show up if all the pieces aren't taken care of. That's psychologically, spiritually, and physically; you show up as a whole being. Women have to get used to the idea."

Ultimately, then, self-care begins with self-worth and self-love. It's built on a foundation of believing in your own importance and the value of your contribution to the world. Your contribution includes your care for others, but caregiving needn't define nor limit you. To use Dr. Fleming's words, you have an "individual zone of genius." You need to discover that zone, embrace it, and structure your life to express it. This isn't putting yourself above or before others, but it is making you equal to them. And fostering your unique contribution enables you to lead, serve, and help others be all that they can be.

Dr. Fleming said, "I don't think many people, even men, to be quite honest, have given themselves permission to set their own journey." In her particular journey as a professional and a mom, Dr. Fleming had no model for how to do both. Her mom hadn't worked outside the family when Fleming was young. And when her parents divorced, young Fleming saw that her mom didn't know what was next for her.

In response, Dr. Fleming resolved early on that she would always make her own plan. Her path would not be a result of what anyone else wanted for her, but what she wanted for herself. There were times, Dr. Fleming admits, when she didn't always stand in the courage of that choice. Many of us can relate to what Dr. Fleming tried to do when she returned to work after a year at home with her first child:

> *When I went back to work, I felt guilty to the point that I took my son's playpen to work. I decided he would be in another office while I was in my office working, and I would visit him. You know that didn't work out, right? People would come in to see my little charmer, and he would talk and play with everybody. And, of course, no one can get any work done like that. I just felt so guilty.*
>
> *One day, I finally said to myself, You can be sad, and you can miss him when you leave him with the caregiver. That's okay. You have chosen the best person to care for him, and you will not feel guilty because you've chosen to be a career woman, mother, and a wife. You can't have it all.*
>
> *I did not allow myself to feel guilty because guilt is the lowest vibration of the human spirit. I would, however, allow myself sadness when I missed things. I still do. I still always strive to allow myself to make choices that feel best for me, my family, and the commitments I've made professionally.*

Today, I can echo Dr. Fleming's words about giving myself permission to set my own path and make the choices I believe are best for me, my family, and the professional responsibilities I've taken on. I was, however, slow to reach this point.

When I interviewed her for this book, Johnnetta Cole, PhD, was in her eighties, having held numerous prestigious positions in her career. To name a few, Dr. Cole was the first woman president of Spelman College, president of Bennett College, and director of the Smithsonian National Museum of African Art. On so many levels, this educator and leader has inspired me and so many others.

In an earlier interview for Diversity Woman Media, Dr. Cole had said, "Any young woman has not only the right but the responsibility to be for herself." She went on to remind us that this doesn't mean that a woman needs to antagonistic toward those who are different. Dr. Cole explained that in opening up to folks whose identities are somewhat different from ours, we not only will have the joy of understanding the realities of people who are different but will also begin to have interesting new ways of looking at ourselves.

In Dr. Cole's youth, "being for herself" didn't equal self-care as we might know it. She has an image of herself stirring a pot at the stove with one baby in the air, another on the floor, all the while thinking of the lecture she wanted to give. The idea of caring for herself didn't enter into her mind.

Even though Dr. Cole's first husband was at least partially supportive of gender equity, so much of what she accomplished came via sleep deprivation.

Times change, of course, and Dr. Cole now sees it as a violation of feminism that she and others like her did not include themselves in the people they cared for. She said, "I took care of my children, my students, and my mentees, but not myself. I now know that we must care for our sisters and ourselves."

One who did care for Dr. Cole as a sister along the way was Dr. Maya Angelou. As Dr. Cole was navigating her second divorce, Dr. Angelou said, "Come and spend the weekend with me. I will cook for you, read poetry to you, and help you move along this journey of healing."

During the final years of my own marriage, I had been laid off, and I started my business as a way to earn an income. Unfortunately, I was a just few years into the business when the economy dropped in 2008.

With the divorce, I became fearful for my financial future. As an entrepreneur in a down economy, without a financial safety net from a spouse, I was scared. A month after my husband and I separated, I started a master's degree in entrepreneurship, thinking I could save my business by getting an educational foundation. If that didn't work, I figured I would be better positioned for another job.

The business survived, but I still worried about relying solely on my income. What if the bottom fell out of the economy again? I decided to pursue my doctorate because the degree would position me as an expert in my industry, with credentials to teach at the college level. I have often called my doctorate my "husband income" because I originally thought of it as a safety net.

Both times I made the decision to pursue an advanced degree, I was in a survival mode. I decided to get my degrees, not because I was pursuing my own path but because I wanted employment security. I wanted to secure the same standard of living I had had when I was married.

During those years, I was living out of fear, and you can imagine the stress that went with that. As a mom, business owner, and doctoral student, I was overloaded with work and responsibilities—and continually stressed out. I was desperate to succeed in my business and my academic pursuits.

Then one day I realized that as important as my business was in helping others and as much as I wanted my doctorate, neither of these things was necessary for me to consider myself successful. As I was talking to my daughter about a problem she was having, I heard myself say, "That doesn't define success."

It was a transformative moment because I suddenly realized what success meant to me. It meant being healthy, happy, and able to provide a good life for my daughter and my mother.

With this realization, the fear I had been carrying for a long time melted away. I realized that there is no reason to be fixated on what I do and what others think I should do or be. To be successful, I don't have to be the president of a company, a gorgeous model, or even a teacher. I could paint white lines on a street or run a cash register and succeed in generating the income I need to be happy, healthy, and provide for my loved ones. That's success by my definition.

Having a clear definition of success profoundly influenced my reaction when COVID-19 hit in March of 2020. The nature of my work has always necessitated being on site and in-person. To produce magazines, we did photo shoots and interviews. We hosted large-scale events and built communities of people. My role had always included speaking engagements.

When COVID-19 hit, I immediately thought, *Well, the methodologies I use to serve my clients are gone*. Yet, I was neither emotionally devastated nor fearful. At no point did I say to myself, *I better go online and start looking for a job as a professor*. I didn't need to do this because I had already formulated plans B, C, and D.

Because my work does not define who I am or my level of success, I'm able to contemplate what-if scenarios and figure out what I'll need to do to continue working toward my own definition of success. This is not to say that being president of Diversity Woman Media is just a job to me. It's the path through which I accidentally discovered my purpose, which is to help other women succeed in their lives and careers.

My initial goal in the business was to help women get better jobs. I began with a vision of helping women learn how to do better in interviews, negotiations, and other strategic areas. While this is a worthy specialty, Diversity Woman Media has come to encompass much more than that.

It wasn't until I began receiving testimonies that I realized what the business and community were becoming. Women began saying, "I went to this conference, and as a result my life has changed"; "I read the interview in your magazine. It gave me what I needed to make a transition in a way I was unable to before"; "Your presentation made an amazing difference in how I view my life"; "Thanks to the conference, I accomplished an elusive goal."

The testimonies helped me see that I was living into my purpose as president of Diversity Woman Media. My purpose is to empower women to reach their highest potential in their lives and careers. Whatever happens with Diversity Woman Media in the future, I will find a way to live into this purpose.

Putting Self-care into Practice

Self-care begins with self-love and embracing the right to choose your own life journey. That's the foundation. It's beyond the scope of this book and my expertise to describe all that self-care involves. I do, however, think we all need to pay attention to what we put in our bodies, how we manage stress, how we move our bodies, who we surround ourselves with, and how we calm our busy minds. I'll be considering these topics in the pages that follow.

As we conclude this chapter, I ask you to make two foundational choices. First, declare yourself worthy of self-care. Even if some part of you struggles, acknowledge the fact that your life path is as important as that of any other human being. It's your responsibility to take care of yourself. No one will do this for you. Ironically, if you fail to take care of yourself, you will limit your ability to care for those you love, at home and at work.

Second, make a commitment to listen to your own body as it tells you what it needs. Edwina Baskin-Bey, MD, an award-winning physician/scientist with twenty-plus years' experience in academia and industry, explained in our interview, "If your body tells you that you need rest, take a rest. If you've been sluggish and need exercise, start moving. If you need time to be alone, even if others around you don't want that, take the time to be alone."

According to Dr. Baskin-Bey, your time alone might include meditation, reading a book, or simply sitting. You need to listen to your body because no one can do that for you.

This physician/scientist says that listening to your body gives you powerful knowledge. She warns you that your body will sometimes surprise you. Sometimes your body will tell you to have an ice cream sandwich (all in moderation) or it will tell you when you've had enough wine. It will even tell you when it's reasonable to have some red meat.

Dr. Michelle Robin, who would remind you to define moderation as 15–20 percent of the time, makes a similar point in a colorful way: "For people to really dial into their well-being, they have to figure out what their body likes. I say we have these little cells standing up on their toes, and when we feed them the right stuff, they are cheering 'Yay, yay, yay.' When we feed them the wrong stuff, they kind of get droopy eyes and they start to flatten."

Your body has a message for you every hour, every day. Are you listening?

Self-care Is an Essential Ingredient in Productivity

In an article called "Wellbeing is Correlated to Higher Performance" on ThriveGlobal.com, Wanda Krause, PhD, points out that seven countries among those with the highest GDP rank have the fewest working hours. This contrasts dramatically with U.S. culture in which we often brag about how many hours we work. But working constantly correlates with lower performance, not higher productivity.

Here's a sampling of the evidence Krause presents in the article to show that well-being—which I think of as whole-person self-care—has to do with productivity:

Sleep. Studies show that increasing your sleep time may improve performance. For example, Cheri Mah, a researcher in the Stanford Sleep Disorders Clinic and Research Laboratory, studied the relationship between sleep and the performance of basketball players at the elite college level. Those players who got more sleep improved their free-throw shooting by 9 percent.

Some of our country's most successful leaders expect their top employees to honor the body's need for sleep. Pat Wadors, LinkedIn's chief human resource officer, says, "When you brag about that (sleeping four to five hours a night), you are telling me that it's ok for you to harm your health and not perform your best at work or at home. Is that something to brag about?"

Purpose. In speaking about the importance of purpose, Krause shares these words of Derek Mowbray, who wrote in the *Training Journal*: "The ingredients for feeling well are clustered around having a purpose in life, feeling personal success and happiness in relation to a number of key elements—relationships, resources, the environment, personal growth, personal control, and other items that individuals feel are important to them."

Exercise. Numerous studies show that exercise is correlated to high performance. Krause points to research on well-being performed by Caroline Mbaabu for Kenyatta University. The results of the research show that those who participate in physical fitness programs can be expected to have "above average performance, lower rates of absenteeism, higher commitment to work, and lower employee turnover."

Creativity. We might not think of creativity as an essential ingredient in productivity. Instead, we think that dogged determination and long hours are key. Not true. Organizational psychologist Benjamin Hardy says, "When you're working, be at work. When you're not working, stop working. By taking your mind off work and actually recovering, you'll get creative breakthroughs related to your work."

Social Support. It's not easy to maintain a balanced approach to self-care and well-being in work cultures where performance goals are always top of mind. Good leaders create a culture where there is a shared understanding of the benefits of well-being. Employees realize that these benefits extend beyond themselves and accrue to their families, teams, and the organization. When benefits are understood, well-being can become a workplace value.

Adapted from Wanda Krause, PhD, "Why Well-Being Has Everything to Do with Productivity," ThriveGlobal.com.

chapter five

Enemy Number One: Stress

COVID-19 meant I needed to make a quick pivot as an entrepreneur whose revenue model relied heavily on public appearances and in-person conferences. At the same time, as a black woman affected by racism and a business that speaks to diversity and inclusion, I wanted to add my voice to the public discussion concerning Black Lives Matter.

This was a highly disruptive time for me—but not all of it was bad. As I said earlier, my identity and sense of success is not heavily tied up in my business. If my company failed, I knew there would be another path and road to success. I also knew I'd find ways to fulfill my purpose of helping other women achieve their own definition of success.

I considered it a privilege to play my part in positive efforts to work toward healing systemic racism in our country. And I had known it was time to increase the digital footprint of Diversity Woman Media; I could hardly resent the nudge.

I had food to eat, my family was healthy, and I had a strong community of personal and professional friends. While there was disruption, I was willing to reset and adapt to changes in the business environment. I wasn't particularly stressed out—at least until I scheduled my first virtual conference for August of 2020.

My most important goal for the conference was to deliver on my company's promise of value. I wanted participants to have the same return on investment (ROI) they would receive at one of our in-person conferences. Other important goals were to increase the visibility and value profile of Diversity Woman Media beyond past offerings.

I felt confident about the content we had to deliver. We have a proven process for identifying relevant, high-quality content for our audience. We had great speakers and panels lined up. What we didn't have was knowledge and control of the technology we needed to deliver our content in a virtual format.

I had lost staff due to COVID-19 challenges, and my remaining team members had to learn the technology we'd be using. The related uncertainty often left me feeling highly stressed and anxious. Although I had used my network to research the best technology available, I kept asking myself, *Did I choose the right digital platform? Can I trust the technology company I hired to manage this?* There was no way for me to be sure, and my brand reputation was on the line.

I reflected a lot about personal and business resilience during this time. I was determined to get through the COVID-19 pandemic without damaging my health or gaining weight. In past high-stress seasons, I gravitated to junk food on the run, adding pounds and increasing feelings of sluggishness and bloat. Now, because I had developed the habit of listening to the messages from my body, I was aware that making poor food choices would only make me feel worse.

From my D.I.E.T. standpoint, I watched my drink and intake (*D* and *I*). In other words, I stayed hydrated and stuck to my healthy food habits while allowing myself the 20 percent indulgence that works for me. I also increased my exercise (*E*). I walked each morning as I usually do, and I added an extra walk during the day. This relieved the physical tension in my body and gave me space to think (*T*) productively.

I addressed my fears of embarrassment and failure by creating backup plans as best I could. I reminded myself that my fifteen years of delivering value would count with my audience even if this one event turned out badly. And I realized that the worst-case scenario would simply entail giving everyone's money back and doing the conference over. Nobody was going to become homeless or die.

With this perspective, I was able to focus on what my team members and I could control. While this didn't relieve all the tension, it did make me feel stronger and more energetic. Plus, I was working productively on what I could control rather than wasting time and energy on worry.

In fact, we didn't wait around until our August conference to reach out with content to our community. Within thirty days of the first shutdown in the U.S., we launched a weekly series of webinars called Moving Forward. In an interview format, renowned experts in diverse fields addressed our community with practical information and strategies to address the stresses and challenges of the pandemic.

The first speaker was Sharon Melnick, PhD, a psychologist and executive coach who helped us understand why we were waking up in the middle of the night and what we could do about it. From there we had psychiatrists, psychologists, doctors, and even a photographer who taught us how to put our best selves forward on Zoom. The Moving Forward webinars were amazing, and each is posted under the Resources tab on our website.

The webinars expanded the resources we offer to clients exponentially, but we didn't stop there. In January of 2020, we launched a weekly webinar series called Wellness Wednesdays. These webinars, also in an interview format, were all about self-care and wellness. Some material from those webinars is included in this book. And once again, the webinars remain available on the website for our community.

Our first virtual conference, with the title of Diversity, Equity, Inclusion, and Belonging, didn't turn out perfectly, but 90 percent of the feedback was positive. Some participants said we knocked the event out of the park! The most important thing: I was totally pleased about what my team and I delivered under the circumstances. The speakers and content were outstanding. I met my most important goal of delivering on my company promise—and I hadn't negatively affected my health.

My team and I learned from the first conference and went on to host two additional virtual conferences during the pandemic. In October 2020, we held our Power Forward conference, which was the capstone event for the Moving Forward webinar series. In April 2020, we held our Self-care, Health, and Wellness conference. This was the capstone event for Wellness Wednesdays. One of the things I'm most proud of is that we officially registered World Women's Wellness Day, observed for the first time on April 30, 2021. I hope you'll join with women everywhere each April 30 to dedicate a day to self-care.

◇◇◇◇◇◇◇◇◇◇

Managing short-term stress, such as a first virtual conference, is hard enough. The bigger factor in our overall health is how we manage chronic stress, the constant in everyone's world today. The human body is hardwired to release a big surge of energy in high-threat, high-stress situations. This is an evolutionary gift from our ancestors. Of course, the nature of high-threat, high-stress situations has changed radically between ancestral days and our own. Unfortunately, our body's way of responding has not kept up with the change.

To survive, our ancestors needed quick influxes of high energy to fight or escape from predators in short-term, intense events. They exerted physical energy in fighting or fleeing, burning up the excess energy the body generated for that purpose. The events were soon over, and the influx of energy needed to survive was depleted at the end of each event. Ancestral bodies went back to normal levels and bodily functions, and all was well.

Our bodies evolved to respond physiologically to stress with an influx of energy—because that's what our ancestors needed to survive. Today, some emergencies, such as fires, car accidents, health traumas, or natural disasters still require a physical as well as a mental response, and our bodies automatically release energy for these situations. These situations, however, are the exception rather than the norm.

We more frequently encounter threats and stress of a different type. The long list includes job insecurity, biased bosses, lack of race and gender equity, fear of failure, aging parents, angry teenagers, medical challenges, and more. None of these stressors call for a physiological response on a par with the threat of a hungry lion. And what good would a surge of short-term energy do in the face of COVID-19 and the variety of threats that came with it? Still, a surge of energy is what we get.

Before we are even conscious of a threat, our bodies perceive the threat and generate an automatic physiological response. We get a rush of hormones operating in complex ways to prepare our bodies for action. Of particular interest here is cortisol, sometimes called the stress hormone.

Cortisol makes energy, in the form of glucose, available to help us fight or flee. All the body's resources get focused on providing energy for a physical battle. Growth, digestion, and other metabolic activities slow down during the crisis.

If the stress is short-term and requires an energetic physical response, everything is good. If the stress is chronic and a physical response is not needed, big problems arise. Chances are you know from experience that chronic elevated cortisol levels (hormonal stress levels) can lead to headaches, heartburn, high blood pressure, insomnia, lower immune function, and other complications. In terms of your general sense of well-being, high cortisol can contribute to irritability, anxiety, and depression.

Jason Fung, MD, author of *The Obesity Code*, describes the complex research in this area. Some of the research has been possible because the drug prednisone is a synthetic version of cortisol. Researchers can study what happens to patients taking prednisone for medical reasons. They can study what happens when those patients stop taking the drug. While acknowledging that more studies in the complex dynamic are needed, Dr. Fung says, "The undeniable fact remains that excess cortisol causes weight gain. And so, by extension, stress causes weight gain—something that many people have intuitively understood . . . Stress contains neither calories nor carbohydrates but can still lead to obesity. Long-term stress leads to long-term elevated cortisol levels, which leads to extra pounds."

To make matters worse, cortisol-related weight gain is associated with increased abdominal fat deposits, where they are especially dangerous to health. That "muffin around the middle" can also kill you.

The big challenge for our mental and physical health is getting rid of the cortisol that is ever-present in our modern lives, especially for women who lead their families, organizations, and communities. The answer comes down, once again, to self-care. The relationship between self-care and stress management is undeniable.

Managing the Stress Cycle

I try to remind myself that not all stress is bad. In fact, we need a certain level of stress to grow. We learn from our experiences, which include challenges, setbacks, experiments, and even failures. For example, my team and I learned from our first virtual conference and went on to produce better ones. From this perspective, stress isn't so much something to be avoided as to anticipate and manage. We can intentionally build our resources and stamina to deal with stress.

One of the most helpful things we can do to prepare ourselves for future stress and strains is to do the necessary work to heal our childhood hurts and past traumas. Unhealed wounds and/or long-term bitter feelings leave us especially vulnerable by influencing the way we interpret events. Such influences can skew otherwise manageable events into debilitating stress episodes for us, complete with floods of dangerous and lingering cortisol. We build stamina by taking care of our unfinished business.

Having lived through a childhood full of drama and trauma, Dr. Michelle Robin says, "You can't take care of yourself unless you heal your heart. Leaders need to do their own work so that they can hold space for the people who entrust themselves to them."

Dr. Robin isn't suggesting wallowing in your past, only that you acknowledge it and look at the gifts that result as well as at the trauma. Acknowledging and releasing your traumas allow you to move on. To do this, some of us need help from therapists, others from good friends. Either way, there's no need for shame.

For me, healing from my divorce involved identifying and changing my own assumptions and behaviors surrounding the relationship as well as facing the pain and responsibilities of my ex-husband. Before I did that work, I could not have imagined how much stronger and more empowered I would be moving forward. Knowing I had a right to discover and pursue dreams of my own was liberating. This knowledge didn't change the demands of graduate school, work, and parenting my daughter, but it certainly changed the way I perceived and responded to those demands. I had a whole new center and sense of identity.

Another thing we can do to build resilience is care for our bodies with good nutrition, regular exercise, and sleep. While this may not be news, it still needs to be said. From a logical standpoint, it just makes sense to burn off excess physical energy from an influx of cortisol with physical exertion.

Wouldn't it be great if all of us had the time and inclination to run ten miles or fight out our frustration in a boxing ring every day? Unfortunately, our schedules are packed, and many of us hate to exercise. In our attempts to keep our weight down, we've gone down the count-calories-and-exercise-more road too many times. It hasn't worked in the past, and we shouldn't expect it to work in the future.

I'm not here to make you feel guilty for the ice cream you eat out of the carton or the exercise you don't get. But I still have to give a plug for regular exercise as a way to build the hardiness you need to weather high-stress situations.

I don't need to tell you that experts agree that regular exercise helps prevent or manage many health problems, including stroke, high blood pressure, type 2 diabetes, depression, anxiety, and many types of cancer. Exercise is proven to improve your cognitive functioning, mood, and energy levels. It also promotes better sleep.

I think I've tried every possible mode of exercise over the years. Most just didn't work for me, but I kept pushing and failing. In fact, the whole idea of exercise was steeped in negativity for me until I read Tom Rath's book *Eat Move Sleep*. My perspective shifted when Rath suggested we strive to add more *movement* of any kind into our lives. The goal is to find movement that you enjoy and add it to your routine.

I'll share my personal journey surrounding exercise in a later chapter. For now, I'll refer back to what I said earlier: taking an outdoor walk works for me on multiple levels. The restrictions that came with COVID-19 blocked some other stress busters, such as hot yoga, which work for me, but even COVID-19 couldn't take away my ability to walk outdoors.

I've learned that for me to remain healthy in body and mind, I must build time for this in my schedule. To be at my best, I need a four-mile walk at least five times a week. It's an essential practice of self-care for me. The movement, the experience of nature, and the space to think are all elements that break the stress cycle for me. I'm not suggesting a daily walk is necessarily the answer for you, but it could be. Some form of movement is right for you, and I encourage you to experiment until you find it.

The same is true of nutrition. One of my reasons for writing this book is to get the word out that eating well can and should be a joy. I want to redefine D.I.E.T. to rid us of the horrible of associations of dogged discipline and deprivation. The list of foods that taste good and boost your health is limitless.

Another way to build stress resilience is to engage in regular spiritual practices. For some, the ideal spiritual practice is prayer; for others, it is meditation or yoga. For still others, it's connecting to a higher purpose or service in life.

With all our responsibilities, it's easy to get tunnel vision and think that our next business proposal or project is the most important thing in life. We can feel the same way about our children's academic achievement or keeping our homes in order. This lack of perspective and connectedness to a higher power drains us and leaves us unprepared for stressors. Taking time to meditate, pray, or practice yoga slows us down. It gets us out of our heads and into our bodies, reminding us to center ourselves in the present moment and breathe. Developing the ability to do this helps us function optimally in general and gives us an indispensable tool when the unexpected hits. Even the simple practice of keeping a daily gratitude journal is one positive step in this direction.

Still another way to build resilience to stress is to invest in community. Historically, men have been more likely to network professionally while women succumbed to pressure to handle responsibilities at home during the same hours.

I'm so proud of the role that Diversity Woman Media plays in changing this trend. We are a growing community of support to help women meet their professional and personal goals. Friendships and community can support you during rough times and provide energy, resources, and practical advice to help you make sound personal and career decisions. When you make time to relax and laugh with members of your community, you do more than give yourself a pleasant break. According to the Mayo Clinic, "A rollicking laugh fires up and then cools down your stress response, and it can increase and then decrease your heart rate and blood pressure. The result? A good, relaxed feeling."

No matter how much hardiness we build in preparation, stressful situations will still hit us hard. When preparing for Diversity Woman Media's first virtual conference, I had to keep my mind and body from being overwhelmed with the stress. The habits of good nutrition I'd developed helped keep my eating under control.

I increased my walking because I had found the type of movement that works best for me. Increasing this movement required an investment of time, but not a sense of discipline—because I enjoyed it. As I walked, I thought a lot about what was happening in my mind. I was able to keep my thoughts in perspective by reminding myself of priorities and the things I could and could not control. I limited my catastrophic thinking by identifying the worst that could happen—and realizing that I could survive that.

Stress and its dangerous companion cortisol are here to stay. Ignoring stress is self-sabotage. Self-care involves assessing your stressors and reducing the ones that are under your control. Self-care also involves building a reservoir of stress resilience. It starts with doing the necessary work to heal traumas from the past, whatever that means for you. It continues with daily habits that keep the mind, body, and spirit in optimal conditions. Don't delay. Take a first step today.

Stress and High-performance Leadership

As leaders, we seek to perform at a high level every day in the face of constant change and pressure. The big question is how?

In an article published in *Harvard Business Review* titled "The Making of a Corporate Athlete," Jim Loehr and Tony Schwartz claim that the problem with most approaches to performance is that they deal with people only from the neck up. In other words, most approaches connect high performance only with cognitive capacity. The authors propose an integrated theory of performance that addresses the body, mind, emotions, and spirit. They have designed a high-performance pyramid, with physical capacity as the foundation, followed by emotional, mental, and spiritual capacity.

This approach grew from the two decades that Loehr and his colleagues spent working with world-class athletes. Eventually, Loehr and Schwartz came to think of high-performing executives as "corporate athletes." To achieve sustained performance at a high level, they posited that executives need to train the way world-class athletes do.

Of particular interest for us is the authors' perspective on increasing physical capacity, the foundation of the pyramid, to combat stress and increase energy. After all, we can push ourselves only so far before we collapse from exhaustion. I know that once my physical energy is depleted, I experience mental fog, irritability, and more.

The key to sustained physical performance, according to these authors, is intentionally managing cycles of stress and recovery. To explain how this works, the authors use the example of weight lifting:

> *Several decades of sports science research have established that the key to increasing physical strength is a phenomenon known as supercompensation—essentially the creation of work-rest ratios. In weight lifting, this involves stressing a muscle to the point where its fibers literally start to break down. Given an adequate period of recovery (typically forty-eight hours), the muscle will not only heal, it will grow stronger. But persist in stressing the muscle without rest and the result will be acute and chronic damage. Conversely, failure to stress the muscle results in weakness and atrophy. In both cases, the enemy is not stress, it's linearity—the failure to oscillate between energy expenditure and recovery.*

Loehr and Schwartz observed that the highest-level athletic competitors create *rituals of oscillation*. Fox example, the best tennis players use precise recovery rituals during the fifteen to twenty seconds between points. These rituals include focusing on the strings of their rackets, adopting a confident posture, and visualizing the next point. Mere seconds in length, the rituals serve to drop the athletes' heart rate by 15 to 20 percent between points. Tennis players who don't practice such rituals between points expend too much energy without recovery. And regardless of their talents and conditioning, it costs them.

What's true for athletes is true for leaders. When Loehr and Schwartz began to work with a director-level executive named Martha Clark, they discovered that she had almost no rest-and-recovery practices in her life. Clark, who ran an office, was raising three small children with her equally high-powered executive husband. Clark was alert and energetic in the mornings, after coffee and a muffin. She worked through lunch and suffered a lag in energy by afternoon. She completed her workday by sheer willpower. Given this schedule and her responsibilities outside of work, Clark had almost no time to herself.

Loehr and Schwartz discovered that while Clark had been a serious athlete in high school and college, she wasn't currently exercising regularly. To improve her energy and performance, the researchers insisted that Clark's first priority needed to be getting in shape. She committed to work out in a gym at one p.m. three workdays a week and over the weekends.

The intentional ritual of stress and recovery helped Clark establish better work and life boundaries and increased her energy and focus in the afternoons. The physical stress of exercise built her up to a point that she can now work fewer hours and get more done. She no longer feels chronically burdened and believes that she is a better boss.

As leaders, we do well to examine our own rest and recovery rituals. Loehr and Schwartz tell us that research by chronobiologists suggests that the body and mind need recovery every sixty to ninety minutes.

What rituals of oscillation can you create to manage your need to recover? In addition to bigger cycles of oscillation such as Clark's, small rituals can make a difference. After all, a tennis player can get recovery results from a fifteen- to twenty-second ritual between points. Maybe a ritual as simple as taking a stretch break or short meditation break between projects or calls can make a difference for you.

Of course, rituals of stress and recovery alone, while essential, aren't enough to build a strong foundation for consistent high performance. Eating and sleeping well are equally important. And would-be corporate athletes need to increase their emotional, mental, and spiritual capacity to build a pyramid of sustained energy and success.

Learn more in Jim Loehr and Tony Schwartz, "The Making of a Corporate Athlete," *Harvard Business Review*.

chapter six

Hydration Is Health: Drink

For most of my life, I judged the state of my health by my weight. If I liked the number on the bathroom scale and my clothes fit well, I considered myself healthy. Of course, there was always a level at which I knew weight alone doesn't determine a person's health. Thin people get heart disease, diabetes, cancer, and other serious diseases. Still, I focused on my weight as my measurement for health, not on the quality of my food, drink, activity, and other factors. Perhaps it was because the one factor that confronted me in the mirror each day was how thin or heavy I looked.

The cardiologist who sparked my decision to make real changes initially talked to me about weight too. He explained the risk my excess weight posed for serious disease and a shortened lifespan. As shocking as the connection between excess weight and a shortened lifespan is, that's not the part that struck home enough to drive change. The cardiologist's words that I still hear echoing in my ears are, "You are an educated woman. You are smart."

As I processed the doctor's words over the next few months, I began to see the huge gap that was obvious to him and had been invisible to me. As an educated woman, I carefully plan my business growth. I put extensive planning into my conferences and draw on experts for the most current research and information. When I want to buy a new car or take a special vacation, I research and plan. I coach women to plan for their next raise and next career step. Why on earth did I fail to educate myself and plan for my current and lifelong health?

I made a big shift after that visit with the cardiologist, but it wasn't simply to go on a diet as I once might have done. While losing weight was obviously going to be necessary, I finally understood that weight was only one piece of the big picture. The bigger shift was to start building awareness and educating myself around whole-person health. My ideas about food were based on ingredients and methods of preparation from my cultural identity. I honestly couldn't say I knew much about how to feed and care for my body.

I'm not a doctor, nutritionist, or fitness expert, but I am now educated—and an educator. That's what compels me to tell my story. My goal is to encourage you to build your awareness and educate yourself based on research and expert knowledge. I've learned that the body is complex, nutrition is complicated, and individuals are unique. Educated women need to invest time and energy to learn the science behind whole-person health and make the commitment to apply that knowledge in ways that make sense to them and their own bodies.

I've organized much of what I've learned on my educational journey about health into D.I.E.T.: *drink, intake, exercise,* and *thinking.* As I write about these areas, I'm not intending to be comprehensive. I know that each of these areas is complex and experts spend lifetimes researching in any one of these areas. I respect and defer to the experts. I'm simply sharing what I've learned through my own research and the interviews I've conducted. The focus of this chapter is *drink.*

My lifetime go-to drink of choice, especially when I felt I deserved a treat, was diet soda. Because it had no calories and no sugar, I thought diet soda was a good choice. When I began to educate myself, however, I learned that consuming diet soda, especially on a regular basis, is a profoundly bad choice.

It seems counterintuitive, right? Surely, artificially sweetened drinks and food must be better for you than the stuff loaded with sugar. Unfortunately, that's not usually the case. When manufacturers take something out of a beverage or food, such as sugar or fat, they add in something else. That something else is typically one or more chemicals. And the chemical additives in food are often worse for us than the sugar they replace.

Diet Soda's Hidden Dangers

In choosing diet soda over sugary sodas as the healthier alternative, I wasn't alone. In *The Obesity Code*, Jason Fung reveals that the consumption of diet sodas increased by more than 400 percent between 1960 and 2000. Today, Fung says, roughly 20 to 25 percent of U.S. adults regularly ingest artificial sweeteners, most often in beverages like diet sodas.

Fung offers a bit of history to help us understand the dangers of artificial sweeteners. In 1879, Russian chemist Constantin Fahlberg had been working on coal-tar derivatives in his laboratory. One evening, when eating a piece of bread with his dinner, the scientist noticed a sweet taste, even though the bread hadn't been baked with any sugar. Upon reflection, Fahlberg realized that he had spilled a compound on his hands. The compound had made everything he touched taste sweet. This event sparked the invention of saccharin, the first artificial sweetener.

Saccharin was originally synthesized as a drink for people with diabetes. Other sweeteners followed, and with them, the potential drawbacks of these substitutes. Some—including cyclamate (think of the brand name Sweet'N Low), aspartame (NutraSweet), and acesulfame potassium (Equal)—have been found to have dangerous or questionable impacts on health. Cyclamate has been banned in the United States because of concerns about bladder cancer.

Sucralose (Splenda) is the most popular artificial sugar today. You'll find it in diet sodas, yogurts, snack bars, breakfast cereals, and other processed foods that are advertised as sugar-free.

Each of these sweeteners was discovered, invented, or somehow created in a laboratory and processed by companies specializing in artificial food additives. Historically, these substances haven't been rigorously tested before being approved for use in our food or drinks.

Food scientists are currently extracting and developing a wide swath of plant-based sweeteners to respond to the outcry about artificial chemicals in our foods. These alternatives include stevia, xylitol, and monk fruit sweetener. The jury is still out on the health impact of most of these substances.

Ingesting questionable chemicals is only one of the dangers of consuming diet sodas. These drinks also disrupt your metabolism in ways that increase your cravings for sweets. In short, a steady diet of drinking diet soda can cause you to gain weight rather than lose it. As a weight loss strategy, diet soda is the ultimate saboteur.

For weight and health management, it's critical to keep your level of insulin low. Higher insulin levels easily lead to insulin resistance, which introduces multiple problems, including a high set-weight that your body will seek to maintain. High insulin levels are a cause behind the yo-yo diet effect that so many of us have experienced. Unfortunately, even sugarless gum or mints cause a spike in insulin.

Fung points to studies showing that sucralose can increase insulin production by 20 percent despite containing no calories and no sugar. Even the consumption of so-called natural sweeteners like stevia can raise insulin levels more than the consumption of regular table sugar.

Artificial sweeteners send confusing signals to the brain that cause the metabolic disruption. Our brains have a reward center that floods with dopamine when we experience something pleasurable, including a delicious meal. While sugar activates the pleasure center of the brain, releasing dopamine, artificial sweeteners do not. No dopamine means no sense of reward. As a result, we continue to crave something sweet. Perhaps you've had the experience of a nagging day-long craving for sweets, even after drinking diet sodas throughout the day. Research confirms your experience, suggesting that consuming no-calorie artificial sweeteners drives the body to want to take in even more calories.

Not So Sweet After All

Table sugar may be better for your body than artificial sweeteners, but that doesn't give you reason to replace diet drinks with regular soda. The average soft drink (twelve-ounce can) contains 150 calories, almost all of which come from some form of sugar, often high-fructose corn syrup. On average, that equates to 35–40 grams of sugar in a single can. A single teaspoon of sugar, equivalent to the contents of a sugar packet you might mix into your tea, is 4.2 grams. Drinking a twelve-ounce sugary soft drink is the equivalent to consuming between seven and ten of those sugar packets—maybe even more—in a single beverage. Just imagining it creeps me out.

While fruit juices are a source of healthy nutrients, they can contain as much sugar as a soda. These naturally occurring fruit sugars are better for you but only in limited amounts. When you consider that it takes four to five oranges to make an eight-ounce glass of juice, it's easy to see why one orange, followed by a glass of water, is a better choice.

Maybe you're skipping the sodas and drinking juices, smoothies, sweetened lattes, or other beverages as a treat. We can all use that caffeinated pick-me-up or a post-workout shake. Just remember that over time, the effect of these drinks can add up fast, especially if you're not watching your caloric intake. Once again, awareness rather than deprivation is important. In this, as in other food choices, I keep the 80/20 rule in mind—good choices 80 percent of the time, a treat or indulgence 20 percent of the time.

If you're not sure where to begin on your health journey, start by paying attention to what you're drinking. Eliminate one soda or diet drink from your daily habit and replace it with water. If you need motivation, read the following message from nutrition expert Christine Ellis. The message was delivered to my inbox as part of the My Fasting Challenge program, for which Ellis is head nutritionist.

> *Water, water, water . . . Water accounts for 60 percent of your body and is essential to every cell. Dehydration lowers your blood volume, so your heart must work harder to pump the reduced amount of blood and get enough oxygen to your cells, which makes everyday activities like walking up stairs and exercise more difficult. When you're well-hydrated, the water inside and outside the cells provides adequate nutrients and removes waste efficiently. Your kidneys use water to filter waste from the*

blood and excrete it in the urine. Keeping yourself hydrated may also help prevent urinary tract infections and kidney stones.

We lose water continually through breathing, perspiring, urinating, and moving our bowels. For our bodies to function properly, we must replenish its water supply regularly through food and drink. Even mild dehydration can deplete our energy and make us tired.

You've heard the general recommendation to drink eight glasses of water a day. As a general rule, easy to remember and measure, it's a reasonable guideline. Your individual water needs depend on many factors, however. Your health, activity levels, and even where you live come into play. Your doctor or nutritionist can help you determine the amount of water that's right for you.

Most healthy people can stay hydrated by drinking water and other fluids whenever they feel thirsty. According to an article by the Mayo Clinic, you might need to modify your total fluid intake based on the following factors:

Exercise. Any activity that makes you sweat calls for extra water to cover the fluid loss.
Environment. Hot or humid weather, which makes you sweat, signals the need for additional fluid.
Overall health. Conditions such as fever, vomiting, diarrhea, bladder infections, and kidney stones, all require additional fluids.
Pregnancy and breast-feeding. Women who are pregnant or breast-feeding, may need additional fluids to stay hydrated.

To make sure your body has the fluids it needs, make water your beverage of choice. It's a good practice to drink a glass of water

- When you wake up each morning;
- With each meal and between meals;
- Before, during, and after exercise;
- Any time you feel thirsty;

- If your urine is dark yellow;
- Each time you drink an alcoholic beverage; and
- When you feel hungry.

Two of the things on this list have made a big difference in my habits and health. The first is to drink a glass of water first thing in the morning, before coffee. I hadn't thought about the fact that our bodies get mildly dehydrated after eight hours without fluid. A glass of water gives my body the fluid it needs to start the day off right.

I've also developed the habit of having a glass of water when I feel hungry throughout the day. I hadn't known that thirst often masquerades as hunger. Symptoms of mild dehydration—headache, fatigue, light-headedness, and difficulty concentrating—can lead us to believe we are hungry. When I experience these symptoms, I drink a glass of water first. Often, that's all I need.

If you don't like water and struggle to drink it, you are not alone. After years of drinking soda, water can seem tasteless and boring. If that describes how it tastes to you, try adding a bit of natural and healthful flavor. Lemon, orange, or cucumber slices can add taste as well as a splash of nutrition. Berries are great too. Some people add herbs and spices, such as mint, lemongrass, ginger, or parsley.

Remember that you can hydrate and fill up at the same time with certain foods. Some vegetables and fruits—including carrots, broccoli, lettuce, cabbage, watermelon, cantaloupe, strawberries, spinach, and celery—are at least 90 percent water. Apples, pears, pineapples, oranges, and grapes also contain high concentrations of water. These are excellent choices for snacks and mealtimes. All these foods deliver multiple benefits. They help you stay hydrated and full while delivering great nutrition. Vegetables are always at the top of the list because they have far less natural sugar in them.

Along with vegetables and fruit, consider adding tea and coffee to your diet. Both are sources of powerful antioxidants. Black tea and black coffee have no calories and no ability to increase your insulin levels. Both can provide a boost and fill you up between meals. Green tea is naturally lower in caffeine than black tea and contains antioxidants known as catechins. Herbal teas, while they contain no tea leaves, are caffeine-free and come in a variety of flavors, including mint, chamomile, hibiscus, lemon balm, and ginger.

Since kicking diet soda to the curb, I know that I'm making healthier choices for myself. In addition to staying adequately hydrated, I'm also limiting my caffeine intake, avoiding spiking my insulin levels, and nourishing my body with water, vegetables, and fruit.

What About Alcohol?

Many people like to kick back with a glass of wine after a rough week—even a fancy cocktail. We know excess alcohol is bad for us, and those fancy cocktails are loaded with calories. But is it okay to enjoy a drink once in a while?

Yes! Once again, good health is not about deprivation. I've made a personal decision not to drink alcohol, but you get to make your own choice. Good health is about making wise choices consistently over time. The following material, adapted from an article called "How Alcohol Effects [sic] Your Body" by Jessica Ball, MS, RD, has been helpful to me.

Alcohol is a diuretic, which means it draws water out of your body. It's a good rule to drink one glass of water for every alcoholic drink you consume. Trying out that new craft beer? Follow it up with a glass of water.

But alcohol has other effects on the body, besides dehydration. Drinking even a single alcoholic beverage per day can raise estrogen levels and increase your body's risk of breast cancer. Additionally, excess or even regular alcohol consumption can negatively impact the health of your gut, pancreas, liver, and brain.

On the other hand, researchers have found some benefits to moderate alcohol consumption—defined as one drink per day for women and two drinks per day for men. This level of alcohol consumption can improve our heart and bone health. Alcohol can also boost good HDL cholesterol in our blood, promoting clean arteries, reducing inflammation, and decreasing the risk of heart attacks and strokes. But those affects only come at this definition of moderate drinking. Heavy drinking, defined as five or more drinks per day, can increase blood pressure and put you at increased risk for heart disease.

Be aware that alcohols are not created equally. While light beers only have around 100 calories, other heavier lagers, IPAs, and malt liquors can have upwards of 220 calories per twelve-ounce serving. And those fancy cocktails can add up quickly. Liqueurs made with ingredients such as cream and sugar can have as many as 170 calories in a single 1.5-ounce shot. Distilled liquors such as rum, vodka, gin, and whiskey have about 100 calories per shot. Mixed drinks often blend several shots with sugary sodas and juices. Translation: that one drink at the bar is more like several combined.

You may have heard that red wine is healthy, but why? The answer is in the grape skins. The skins of the grapes are separated from the fruit to make white wine, but with red wine, the skins remain throughout the fermentation process. Those skins contain antioxidants; therefore, red wine has more of these than white wine. Antioxidants help protect your cells from damage and are thought to be essential in the fight against cancer and other diseases, such as diabetes and dementia.

When it comes to alcohol, it's perfectly fine for most people to enjoy a drink now and then. Moderation, of course, is key. Be wary of the mixed drinks from the bar. When in doubt, opt for wine over beer, and remember to drink a glass of water to rehydrate!

Learn more in Jessica Ball, MS, RD. "What Happens to Your Body When You Drink Alcohol," EatingWell.com.

chapter seven

You Are What You Eat, and More: Intake

If I could have you remember only one thing I've learned about habits that lead to health and productivity, it's that healthy eating is not about deprivation. For most of my life, I didn't understand this. It was—and still is—a learning process for me. Looking back, however, I can see I've come a long way. For example, my friends and I still laugh at an experience we shared when I just beginning my transition to eating well.

We had been at a large event in Washington, D.C., and were meeting some clients for dinner. I had just begun experimenting with intermittent fasting (more on this later) and felt famished. I couldn't wait to eat. I had skipped breakfast, lunch, and all snacks by then, and while the others were ordering cocktails, I ordered a coffee and quickly opened the menu, ready to reward myself with a satisfying meal.

To my dismay, everything on the menu was fried, full of sugar, or loaded with cream. The restaurant was more of a bar, and the menu was quite limited. I don't recall this part, but my friends say I threw the menu into the middle of the table and said, "Oh my God, I don't see anything in there that I want. I don't see anything I can eat!"

The group went suddenly quiet, with my friends thinking, *Hold on a minute. Sheila is always nice, always accommodating. What's going on?*

I confessed that I had been fasting and was anticipating a good meal. My friends offered to go to another restaurant, but I refused, drinking coffee and water while they ate their fill. I was miserable until I could reach a place where they served healthier foods that were allowed in my diet.

My perspective today is totally different. I know that intermittent fasting has been a part of health and religious traditions from the beginning of time. While it takes the body time to adjust to fasting, it needn't be a miserable experience. In fact, I regularly practice intermittent fasting and don't feel deprived at all. I won't say I'm never hungry, but I don't experience a gnawing hunger or long hours of discomfort that feel like deprivation.

I also know that people who practice good nutrition can enjoy eating at social events as much as anyone else. I still remember how exciting it was when I started discovering lists of foods that nourish the body—foods that experts encourage us to eat in satisfying quantities. We've always been told what food we should stay away from; it's wonderful to learn about foods we should enjoy.

I've learned that I crave certain foods because I was born and raised on them. Cultural messages around love, celebration, and food abound. I used to believe it wasn't a party unless there was cake. I used to believe life would be tasteless without macaroni and cheese and fried chicken. These are the ultimate comfort foods from my childhood.

As an adult, I ate certain foods regularly because they were easy to make or easy to grab on the way home from work. Most of my food consumption was on autopilot. Often, after a long day, I would simply eat out of habit, not really tasting or enjoying the food. Even so, I would growl like a bear coming out of hibernation if you tried to take those foods from me.

I've learned that people who live the most satisfying lives are intentional, and they make room for celebration and indulgence. My personal menu is no longer those five or six go-to items that I loved. I've expanded what I can eat and enjoy. I have an abundance of appetizing dishes in my repertoire. I expanded my options and my enjoyment of food. I can find something to enjoy on any menu in any restaurant.

When it comes to fried chicken or macaroni and cheese, I have absolutely eaten both since I've made my healthy transition—and I will eat both again. Honestly, these foods have lost a bit of their appeal; they just don't send me over the top anymore. Perhaps it's because I've come to enjoy a green salad topped with avocado, shrimp, and veggies even more.

Once again, I follow the 80/20 rule, which has proven to be a magic formula for me. With this ratio, I can indulge without feeling guilty or obsessing about one meal ruining my health. I can even celebrate in a bar with a limited menu, knowing that I'll be okay even if I eat a meal that isn't particularly healthy. While I typically plan ahead and patronize restaurants that offer a variety of options, I can enjoy myself at any party or restaurant, no matter what is served.

Here's an important point. When I do eat foods that are deep fried, high in refined carbohydrates (white bread, cakes, cookies, crackers, cereal, etc.), or loaded with sugar, I notice that my sense of pleasure is short-lived. Soon after ingesting such foods, I feel sluggish and somewhat uncomfortable. On the other hand, a piece of dark chocolate or a well-prepared piece of fresh fish leaves me feeling energetic and great.

◇◇◇◇◇◇◇◇◇

I think it's fair to say that my peers and I were not only taught, but indoctrinated, in certain principles surrounding nutrition. Chief among them is that weight management is a straightforward matter of calories in versus calories out. In other words, if you want to lose weight, you simply need to take in fewer calories on a regular basis than you burn off by your daily activities and exercise. It's basic math.

While this premise has extraordinary sticking power, scientists now know that it is false. In fact, weight is largely determined by hormones that seek to keep the body in a homeostatic state. The hormones include insulin, which converts the sugar in our food into energy; leptin, which signals a sense of fullness and encourages the body to stop eating; ghrelin, which signals hunger and pushes the body to eat; and cortisol, which is the stress hormone we discussed earlier. These hormones interact among themselves and with other factors in complex ways. For example, the amount of ghrelin in your system is influenced by how much sleep you get.

In addition to learning the calories in versus calories out principle, I grew up believing that all fats were bad. I was taught that a diet of artery-clogging fatty foods was a sure path to heart disease. The American Heart Association endorsed this idea, and food manufacturers went wild creating reduced-fat products. Unfortunately, manufacturers added an inexhaustible list of additives to the food to replace the flavor that went down the drain with the fat. Current research shows that a variety of healthy fats are good for you and can help you feel full. Why not help your body function well while feeling satisfied?

I was long past my formative years before I heard the term microbiome. According to the National Institute of Environmental and Health Sciences (NIEHS), "The microbiome is the collection of all microbes, such as bacteria, fungi, viruses, and their genes, that naturally live on our bodies and inside us."

Given that there are as many microbes as there are cells in the body, building a healthy microbiome is essential to our health. Scientists are a long way from fully understanding how the microbiome works. At the very least, they've come to understand that strong antibiotics kill off good and bad microbes. This is why we now hear so much about probiotics and gut health. Consider this material from the NIEHS:

> *Although microbes require a microscope to see them, they contribute to human health and wellness in many ways. They protect us against pathogens, help our immune system develop, and enable us to digest food to produce energy. Some microbes alter environmental chemicals in ways that make them more toxic, while others act as a buffer and make environmental chemicals less toxic...*
>
> *Differences in the microbiome may lead to different health effects from environmental exposures and may also help determine individual susceptibility to certain illnesses. Environmental exposures can also disrupt a person's microbiome in ways that could increase the likelihood*

of developing conditions such as diabetes, obesity, cardiovascular diseases, allergies, and inflammatory bowel disease.

As I have worked on this chapter about intake, I've been keenly aware of how much is beyond my expertise. I must leave all but the most superficial discussion of hormones and the microbiome to the experts.

I feel confident, however, in writing about my own journey, including my increasing awareness and the shift to put what I learned into play. The changes I've made in intake (the *I* in D.I.E.T.) fall into the following three actions:

- Increasing the quality of the food I eat. I'm learning to expand my intake of foods that support health while avoiding those that harbor harmful additives and chemicals or strip away my good bacteria.
- Decreasing my exposure to toxins. I'm learning to avoid unintentionally introducing toxins into by body through skin care and cleaning products.
- Paying attention to *when* I eat as well as *what* I eat. In researching intermittent fasting, I've discovered that choosing healthy foods, while essential, is only one part of the health and weight equation. Managing when I eat that food is equally important.

While writing this book, I interviewed Mindy Pelz, DC, founder of Family Life Wellness. This expert's interest in health began when she was nineteen years old and suffering from a debilitating case of chronic fatigue syndrome. A traditionally trained physician recommended that young Mindy drop out of college and experiment with a variety of medications to see which might work for her. Dissatisfied with that approach, Mindy's mother took her to a holistic medical doctor who recommended an entirely different approach. He recommended taking everything out of Mindy's diet except for meat and vegetables.

At nineteen, Mindy went from a diet of pizza and beer to one of meat and vegetables. Within three weeks, her energy returned, and the brain fog she had been experiencing went away. The young woman promptly returned to college and graduated.

Mindy Pelz went on to study and practice as a doctor of chiropractic and enjoyed helping patients prevent medical problems. After roughly ten years, she realized that her work was falling short of treating the whole person. She began to educate her patients on the importance of nutrition in overall health. Today, Dr. Mindy is a respected figure in the alternative health world, host of one of the leading science podcasts, *The Resetter Podcast*, and author of three best-selling books.

In our extensive interview, Dr. Mindy explained how she views the body:

> *The body is an intelligent, self-healing machine, but we haven't been taught how to tap into its healing power. From the minute we are born, we are told that health comes from the outside. We are told that we need to be treated from the outside by a vaccination, doctor, supplement, or pill. While I don't oppose helpful intervention, we need to be careful of the mindset that ignores the body's own drive and wisdom to heal. We need to be aware that we are surrounded by interferences that slow the body's natural healing. We need to remove the interferences that block the miracle we were meant to be. The word that best embodies that for me is reset.*

Building on this perspective and through extensive study, Dr. Mindy has a wealth of knowledge to share. As her information informs the three Intake categories of my own journey, Dr. Mindy's advice is sprinkled throughout this chapter.

Increase the Quality of Food

For me, one of the first steps toward health was examining my habits and go-to foods. So much of what I ate was determined by habit, convenience, and unexamined beliefs about love, comfort, and indulgence. When I stepped back and gave whole, natural foods a chance, I discovered that they taste much better than the convenience foods I had turned to for most of my adult life. When I slow down enough to taste it, a juicy apple or crunchy bite of fresh arugula is delicious!

Dr. Mindy says, "The first and most important thing is that we put quality food in our bodies. Strive to eat chemical-free food."

Many health experts recommend a simple way to move in this direction: shop the perimeter of the supermarket. You'll find produce, meat, and dairy—all fresh and perishable foods—on the perimeter of the store. These are the foods the body needs to thrive.

In the center aisles, you'll find crackers, pasta, cookies, cereal, drinks, etc. These foods are processed and laden with chemicals. Unfortunately, the FDA does a poor job of regulating the additives and chemicals in these foods.

When you consider buying a product from a center aisle, experts recommend that you read the nutritional label first. Here's the simple rule: if you can't pronounce or identity an ingredient, don't buy the product. In fact, as a rule, choose any food that doesn't require a nutritional label, such as a vegetable, over a food that does.

Finally, don't be taken in by the "all fat is bad" doctrine you may have heard for most of your life. Josh Axe, DC, DNM, CNS, says the following:

> *A good rule of thumb is to steer clear of highly processed fats that are pumped full of additives and unhealthy ingredients. Refined vegetable oils, processed meats, and snack foods like chips, crackers, and baked goods are generally high in disease-causing, artery-clogging trans fats that should be avoided at all costs.*
>
> *Conversely, the key to finding healthy fats to eat is to look for ingredients that are unprocessed and naturally high in fats. Avocados, full-fat dairy, olive oil, and fatty fish are just a few foods with healthy fats that can benefit your health.*

Imagine: experts are discovering that full-fat dairy products, including butter, are better than low- or reduced-calorie foods. In her cookbook, *The Reset Factor Kitchen*, Dr. Mindy has a recipe for buttered coffee!

Decrease Exposure to Toxins

According to Dr. Mindy, the toxins we are exposed to, whether in our food or the environment, disrupt the natural intelligence and self-healing processes of our bodies. If you begin to read the labels on food packages, it won't take long to realize that we regularly consume chemicals.

The longer the shelf life of a food, the more likely it's loaded with chemicals. The more altered the food from its natural state (as in reducing fat or sugar), the more likely the food has chemical additives to make it taste better. Most of our processed foods also contain chemical dyes. The chemicals in our food can create many health problems, including headaches, hyperactivity in children, asthma, anxiety, and cancer.

The point of the various cleanses we read about is to remove these chemicals from the body, some cleanses being more reasonable than others. Dr. Mindy focuses on reset—allowing the body to get back to its own intelligence, beginning by removing the chemical interferences from our food.

Of course, food is not the only source of dangerous toxins. Laundry and cleaning products are an obvious concern. Other sources are well hidden.

I remember my shock when I first learned that nearly all deodorants contain aluminum, and I was absorbing a toxin directly through my skin every day. I became fearful that my cookware and beverage cans were also leaching aluminum into my body. With some research, I learned that cookware and aluminum cans are sealed, coated, or lined in ways that prevent leaching. Aluminum foil, however, is not.

Putting aluminum foil directly in contact with food is unsafe. I grew up cooking the Thanksgiving turkey in an aluminum pan and wrapping the leftovers in aluminum foil. Didn't we all?

Even more ubiquitous than aluminum foil is plastic and polystyrene (Styrofoam). You've likely heard that BPA in plastic is bad for you. It is one of a number of chemicals known as endocrine disrupters that interfere with the body's hormones. These chemicals are linked to developmental, reproductive, immune, and other problems.

When I first started to educate myself on toxins, I was overwhelmed and dismayed to learn that top-brand skincare and beauty products are loaded with chemicals that the skin absorbs. The aluminum in antiperspirants is just one example. Studies show that women who use antiperspirants for years are likely to have a buildup of aluminum in their breast tissue. No scientific link between this buildup and breast cancer has been established, but I don't want to take a chance.

I was grateful to learn about the app Think Dirty and its website: www.ThinkDirtyapp.com. The app enables you to scan a product for safety information before you purchase it. Consider scanning the shampoo, moisturizer, and facial wash currently in your bathroom to see if they contain toxins. You are likely to be surprised.

When and **What** You Eat

I have explained how my initial forays into fasting were less than ideal experiences. Today, I practice fasting for eighteen hours on most days and believe the practice helps me manage my weight. What's important is that this practice, known as intermittent fasting, is much more than a weight management strategy. I remember hearing someone describe intermittent fasting as a health strategy with the benefit of weight loss. My sense of well-being and productivity is soaring, and I believe fasting is a significant contributor.

Although fasting has been practiced all over the world for religious and health reasons, researchers are only now learning how it works to heal the body. It fits with the intelligent design of the body that Dr. Mindy speaks of.

If you want to delve into the science behind intermittent fasting, you'll find Mindy Pelz, DC, Jason Fung, MD, and Gin Stephens are excellent resources. Refer to the notes at the end of the book. For our purposes here, I'll try to give a quick overview.

Simply put, our bodies convert the food we eat into blood glucose (a form of sugar) that provides the fuel we need to function. Our bodies release the hormone insulin to process the blood glucose. In her book *Fast. Feast. Repeat.*, Gin Stephens explains how the process is designed to work:

> *Insulin is a storage hormone, so it helps our cells take in the glucose from our blood and store it temporarily in the liver and muscles (as glycogen) or, once the glycogen stores are full, the excess can be converted and stored as fat.*
>
> *Over time, the levels of glucose in your blood go down (thanks, insulin, for doing your job!) and the pancreas then releases the counter-regulatory hormone glucagon, which signals your body to release glycogen from the liver to raise blood glucose levels so your body (and brain) can function properly. As your glycogen stores are used up, your body next starts tapping into some of the fat you've stored on your body for times like these. Your body produces ketones from your stored fat, which is a fabulous fuel for your brain in the absence of glucose.*

This is the wonderful, intelligent design of the body we've inherited from our ancestors. One of the reasons we have an obesity epidemic in our country, as well as a proliferation of many diseases, is because our current eating and drinking behaviors disrupt this elegant process.

Think, for example, about the changes in food and drink habits in recent history. In the 1950s and '60s, families typically ate three meals a day, with an additional after-school snack for kids. Blood sugar levels rose and fell accordingly, including a twelve-hour stretch overnight. The body used the low insulin periods to perform other functions, including repairing damaged cells.

Today, most people eat three meals, plus multiple snacks, and/or graze all day long. Vending machines full of drinks and snacks are everywhere, and people take in calories and release insulin all day and all night long. If you are sipping an energy drink or iced coffee with milk over an extended period at your desk or in your car, your body is releasing insulin with each new sip. The same is true when you snack on potato chips or eat bowls of ice cream in front of the television before going to bed. Even sugar-free drinks and gum trigger the release of insulin.

The production of all this insulin leads to insulin resistance, the decreased ability to process and use blood sugar efficiently. And, if the body is constantly full of blood sugar, it has no need to use stored fat—and there's no downtime to perform other functions or repairs. Diseases such as type 2 diabetes, metabolic syndrome, cardiovascular disease, certain cancers, and Alzheimer's disease are all linked to insulin resistance.

The goal of intermittent fasting is to align our eating habits with the bodies we have, which happen to be the same bodies as our cavemen and cavewomen ancestors. Our ancestors did not have access to food all hours of the day as we do. In fact, at times our ancestors would go days without eating at all.

We tend to feel light-headed, weak, or mentally sluggish after several hours without food. This is more about our habits and expectations than our bodies' experiences.

Here's why: When our ancestors hadn't eaten for days, they needed to be mentally sharp to hunt or find food. The body responded in the way it needed to survive. It tapped into an alternate energy system, deriving energy from fat rather than the glucose in food just coming in. Science indicates that fasting for a certain amount of time causes the body to flip a metabolic switch and tap into alternative energy. Dr. Mindy says, "Ketones are a sign that you have tapped into this energy system, and they make you mentally clear."

People practice intermittent fasting in a variety of ways. Some eat within a window of eight or six hours, as I do. It took a while for my body to adjust, but I don't struggle with it now. I do notice that when I eat refined carbohydrates during my window, I notice hunger sooner. If I eat proteins, healthy fats, vegetables, and fruits, I'm typically comfortable during my fast.

Some intermittent fasters eat one meal a day, spaced out over a few hours. Still others practice longer fasts of twenty-four, thirty-six, or more hours, mixing it up. Science indicates that different metabolic switches are triggered at different fasting lengths. The longer fasts not only trigger the body to burn fat, they also trigger the body to make various repairs. Again, this is the natural intelligence of the body, which we disrupt with our constant intake of food and beverages.

I'm in no position to advise you about your practice of fasting. Once again, I encourage you to educate yourself with reputable sources. And, of course, speak with your doctor before you start any health program, especially if you have underlying conditions. The point I want to communicate is that *when* you eat is as important as *what* you eat.

Eating for Nutrients and Satisfaction

Keeping our appetites in check is always a challenge. If you tend to reach for foods that leave you wanting more, try swapping them out for alternatives that make you feel fuller for longer.

An article published by the Mayo Clinic explains the concept of energy density, and a strategy that can help you lose weight without constantly always feeling hungry. "Simply put, energy density is the number of calories (energy) in a specific amount of food. High energy density means that there are a lot of calories in a little food. Low energy density means there are few calories in a lot of food."

To feel full while cutting down on calories, choose food with a low energy density. For example, the article compares one cup of raisins to one cup of grapes. One cup of raisins has about 434 calories. Grapes have a low energy density—one cup of grapes has about 82 calories.

Three main factors contribute to rendering a food high or low in energy density: water, fiber, and fat.

Water. Vegetables and fruits do a great job of helping you feel full because most have a high percentage of water along with lots of fiber. Water provides volume without a lot of calories. According to the article, a grapefruit is about 90 percent water and 37 calories. Raw carrots are about 88 percent water and just 25 calories. To help you feel fuller longer, consider snacking on raw vegetables and adding more of them to your salads. Also add more cooked vegetables to soups and stews. If you are going to have dessert, consider fresh berries on a small scoop of ice cream or Greek yogurt.

Fiber. Vegetables, fruits, and whole grains all contain fiber. These foods provide volume and an additional bonus. Because foods that are high in fiber take longer than other foods to digest, you feel full for longer after your meal. Along with increasing your vegetable intake, try some air-popped popcorn for a snack or a bowl of oatmeal topped with blueberries for breakfast. (Just remember to use the whole grain oatmeal rather than the instant packet, which has been stripped of its fiber.) Experiment with brown rice and other whole grains. Grain-based entrees (usually called bowls) are now available at many restaurants.

Fat. Unlike vegetables, fruits, and grains, fats are high in energy density. A small serving of full fat dairy and some meats pack a high calorie punch. As we've discussed, expert opinions about fat are changing. Some fats are reported to help you feel full while others are reported to make you soon feel hungry. That debate is beyond the scope of this book. The Mayo Clinic article recommends you "include small amounts of healthy monounsaturated and polyunsaturated fats in your diet. Nuts, seeds, and oils, such as olive, flaxseed and safflower oils, contain healthy fats."

The basic concept of energy density is easy to understand and follow. If you want to feel full, eat foods that contain lots of volume and few calories. Vegetables, fruits, and whole grains are, as they have always been, your friends.

Learn more at "Weight Loss: Feel Full on Fewer Calories," MayoClinic.org.

chapter eight

Enjoy How You Move: Exercise

For most of us, our first experience with exercise, good or bad, was in school. In grade school, I loved playing kickball outdoors with my friends. By high school, I was on the cheerleading squad and ran for my school's track and field team. I was an athlete, through and through. I even broke the city and county records for my 110-meter hurdle.

I had so much energy back then. Chances are you had high energy as a child too. Think of all the things you had to accomplish throughout the course of a school day: you got up, went to classes, participated in extracurricular sports or activities, came home, did your homework, ate dinner, enjoyed free time in the evening, and then got a good night's sleep. It was a full day.

I don't remember feeling overly tired or giving in to stress eating during that time of my life, and I had no problem staying active. I continued cheerleading in my freshman year of college. But over time, staying active became less of a priority for me.

As the years wear on, even those of us who were active as children and adolescents tend to slow down. Once we cross the threshold into adulthood, we feel pressure to shift our priorities. We're taught that playtime is over. As a result, play and movement become secondary to other responsibilities: advanced education, career, family, professional development, and so on.

It's easy to let this happen. In college, we have new routines and higher expectations to meet in our academic and social lives. That's where the freshman fifteen comes in, that initial fifteen-pound weight gain that so many students experience when they are away from home for the first time.

We get used to staying up late and pulling all-nighters studying, reaching for pizza instead of a nutritious meal, and maybe drinking some carb-heavy alcoholic beverages. It's no wonder we're so prone to weight gain when we reach college and beyond!

In college and as a young professional, I was no longer running track and field, but I had additional hurdles to face. My routines and responsibilities changed again when I entered the workplace and began raising a family. During that period of my life, I let many other things take precedence over my self-care. If I had any free time at all, I didn't want to spend it exercising—something I saw by then as a punishment more than a reward for my body. Instead, weight loss and self-care became contingent upon a specific event: the high school reunion, the wedding, the cruise, or the family vacation. I focused on losing weight to look good in the photos (or a particular outfit) rather than with an eye to how I felt or functioned.

If you read the title of this chapter and groaned, don't worry. My goal isn't to urge you to sign up for an expensive gym membership and insist you fit a grueling workout into your already packed schedule. Instead, I want to encourage you to shift how you think about exercise. In fact, I want you to think of the *E* in the D.I.E.T. formula as *enjoyment*. Finding movement that you can enjoy has benefits for the body and the mind. When I redefined exercise as movement I enjoy, everything changed for me.

Small Changes Bring Big Results

According to Tom Rath, in his *New York Times* bestseller *Eat Move Sleep*, "Sitting is the most underrated health threat of modern times." Calling it a subtle epidemic, Rath compares our habits of sitting at work and during leisure with the more active lifestyles of our ancestors. Whether we go back to our hunter-gatherer ancestors or the farmers of more recent history, the difference is enormous.

Today, more jobs than ever can be done from the comfort of our homes. And when we're done with work, many of us park ourselves in front of the television until it's time to go to bed. It's no surprise that sitting in front of a computer all day, followed by binge-watching a show all evening, will not help us meet our weight and fitness goals. We know this, and yet so many of us live these sedentary lifestyles. So how bad can it be?

Rath suggests that we consider the perspective of Marc Hamilton, a professor and diabetes researcher, who claims that sitting for extended periods of time is as bad for our health as smoking or spending too much time in the sun.

Not all researchers support this comparison, but many acknowledge that exercising for thirty minutes a few times a week is not enough to reverse the physical damage that comes from endless hours of sitting.

As Rath explains:

> *The act of sitting literally makes your backside bigger. When researchers studied MRI images of muscle tissue, they found that sitting around for long periods of time could put pressure on cells and cause the body to produce more fat than it usually would. This research suggests that when force is placed on a specific area in the body for an extended time, it causes fat tissue to expand. So even if you exercise regularly, sitting for many hours encourages fat cells to congregate near your rear.*

In addition to your fat cells, your enzymes, cholesterol, and sugar levels are all negatively affected by excessive sitting. Unfortunately, there is no formula that describes a ratio of hours sitting to minutes or hours of exercise needed to reverse the effect. In fact, the answer is not so much through exercise but through activity.

The secret is to break up the time sitting by standing, stretching, walking, or some other movement. Even a few minutes of walking can counterbalance the effects of excessive sitting. Standing and moving every twenty to thirty minutes makes a difference.

If your work involves hours in front of the computer, consider brief periods of moving or stretching as an investment in your health. If you lead others or participate on a team, encourage them to do the same. You might even consider investing in a modular desk that can be raised or lowered. If you work remotely, consider throwing in a load of laundry or vacuuming a room between calls. Anything that breaks up your time in a chair is good for you.

The Magic Combination: Exercise and Productivity

As I moved up the corporate ladder and later when I started Diversity Woman Media, I focused on my career goals. I thought that I was doing the right thing by concentrating on all my quarterly and yearly objectives. But without fitting movement into the equation, it turns out I was actually doing myself—and my career—a disservice.

When I began genuinely taking care of myself, which included eating nutritious food and incorporating regular movement into my routine, I was amazed at how the pounds fell off, my energy level increased, and my productivity soared. Research confirms my experience.

A number of studies cited in *Harvard Business Review (HBR)* found that exercise isn't only good for your body—it also benefits the mind. Exercise has been shown to improve concentration, sharpen memory, increase mental stamina and learning ability, enhance creativity, lower stress, and even elevate mood. These qualities can help us boost our performance on the job and in life.

The key, of course, is making time for exercise. I used to feel that between work, family, and other obligations, I didn't have time to work out. The truth is that I had the time—I just didn't want to make exercise a priority. In an *HBR* article called "Regular Exercise Is Part of Your Job," Ron Friedman, PhD, and award-winning psychologist writes:

> *Instead of viewing exercise as something we do for ourselves—a personal indulgence that takes us away from our work—it's time we started considering physical activity as part of the work itself. The*

alternative, which involves processing information more slowly, forgetting more often, and getting easily frustrated, makes us less effective at our jobs and harder to get along with our colleagues.

In other words, exercise isn't just something that benefits our physical health and stamina. The time we carve out for physical fitness informs how we show up in the boardroom or during the video conference call. I know from my experience that when I'm getting enough exercise, I'm also giving myself the space to think through problems I may be facing. This space helps me see things from different perspectives. There's no doubt about it: when I regularly engage in self-care, including exercise I enjoy, I am far more energetic and productive than when I don't.

Harness the Power of Habits

For many of us, the first step in building exercise we enjoy into our lives is overcoming the mental blocks we've constructed. These blocks can take on many forms, but most often they're excuses—we don't have the money, the time, or the knowledge when it comes to exercising. And it's so much easier to not make a change, no matter how positive the change might be.

The most common reason people give for failing to exercise is lack of time. Dr. Nancy O'Reilly pushes back, "If you don't have time to exercise, you don't have time to be healthy."

We don't make exercise a priority because at some level we don't like it, think it's just too hard to exercise consistently, or don't believe the research results that indicate how crucial exercise is to health and productivity.

I've discovered that the people whose lifestyles I most admire build habits and routines into their lives. The habits ensure these individuals fit the activities they value into their schedules. Exercise is just one element of a positive routine. The people I interviewed for this book had routines or habits surrounding all elements of D.I.E.T. For example, they may start every day with a large glass of water and place another on their desk to sip throughout the day.

When Dr. Shanequa Fleming told me about her morning routine, she was careful to say that she gives herself permission to vary the routine. Most mornings, however, Dr. Fleming is up at five a.m. and begins her day with five to ten minutes of gratitude. Beginning the day with gratitude is non-negotiable for Dr. Fleming because it opens her day with thankfulness and possibility.

Dr. Fleming follows her time of gratitude with some type of exercise. It might be walking on a treadmill, doing some stretching or Pilates, or practicing yoga—something that gets her blood flowing. Dr. Fleming says, "I didn't used to be regimented about it, but I discovered that when I started my day without taking time to stretch and move, I felt stiff throughout the day. I was always trying to stretch my neck. When I take time in the morning to stretch, I feel better all day."

Personal trainer Shaun Canoy has found that time spent praying is an essential part of each day for him. He also journals on a regular basis. These practices refresh him mentally in much the same way that exercise refreshes him physically. The consistency, he says, has a power. For example, Canoy says, "If you engage in one positive habit of doing ten jumping jacks every day at ten a.m., it encourages you to develop other positive habits as well. Because of your success in that one habit, you may decide to make ten sales calls each day at eleven a.m. There's a domino effect as you consistently add positive habits to your life."

Stephen Guise, author of *Mini Habits: Smaller Habits, Bigger Results*, would agree. The book begins with Guise's ten-year attempt to meet his goal of regularly exercising. He had occasional motivational bursts that lasted a couple of weeks before petering out. Nothing he tried seemed to stick. As we all know from experience, willpower and self-discipline aren't always enough to accomplish our goals.

One January day, Guise made the decision to start again with a thirty-minute workout, as he had many times before. This time, however, he found he just couldn't begin. It wasn't the effort required to put in one workout that kept Guise from starting; it was awareness of the total amount of work needed to reach his fitness goal. He was intimidated and overwhelmed by the sheer amount of work before him. That's where the resistance lay. Why start when the mountain you must climb is so high?

Even in the face of discouragement, something shifted in Guise that day. Stemming from a thought process he credits to the book *Thinkertoys: A Handbook of Creative Thinking Techniques* by Michael Michalko, Guise challenged himself to do one push-up—just one. Given that the energy and commitment to do one push-up was nearly nonexistent, Guise got in position and did his push-up. Then, since he was already in the position, Guise did a few more.

Guise's muscles hurt after the push-ups because he was so out of shape, but he wondered what would happen if he challenged himself to do one pull-up. It turns out he did a few pull-ups and felt good about them.

That day, Guise got through a thirty-minute workout by setting micro goals: ones that were so easy to accomplish that they met with none of the internal resistance that would typically stop him before he even began.

Guise refers to that one push-up as his golden push-up. Throughout that whole year, Guise continued to drive himself for that one push-up per day. Most days he did more. He explains the results like this:

> *I noticed two things. First, just a few push-ups a day does make a difference in how you feel, physically and mentally. I felt stronger and my muscles were better conditioned. Second, I realized that exercise was becoming habitual, even with such a wimpy challenge. I was doing something every day. Regular workouts were becoming easier.*

Guise began to experiment with and research the power of habits. He discovered that while his method of "stupid small" steps won't help you undo bad habits such as smoking or gambling, it will help you form all kinds of positive habits to meet your goals. For example, let's imagine you want to be an author. If you'd like to write 3,000 words a day, Guise suggests you require yourself to write 50 words a day instead. If that's too difficult, require even fewer words. Pick a number that is too easy to resist—and meet that goal every day.

Approaching your goals this way, as Shaun Canoy told us, creates a domino effect. Guise explains it this way, "The power of the *Mini Habits* system is in the application, mindset, built-in positive feedback looping, naturally increasing self-efficacy, and of course, leveraging small steps into habits." The dynamic can have surprisingly big results:

- You are likely to do bonus reps after you meet your mini requirement. This is because simply getting started reduces your resistance to something you want to do anyway.
- Once you have the routine, it's easier to do more of whatever mini habit you choose. You just do more repetitions.
- Your repeated success in completing your mini challenge will create positive feelings and increase your motivation. These feelings are in direct contrast to the negative feelings you have when you fail to meet your goals.

When you're just beginning to add movement into your daily routine, it can feel daunting. If you feel overwhelmed, start small. Those little movements can add up to big health wins later on.

Four Ways to Get Moving

As I mentioned earlier in the book, one of the ways that I learned to combat stress was to take a daily walk. By moving around and being outside, I was able to increase my physical fitness and gain new insights into what was going on in my life. Later, when COVID-19 shuttered my favorite hot yoga studio, my daily walks helped me avoid the feeling of claustrophobia that came with sheltering in place.

I walk four miles as a daily habit and listen to audiobooks as I go. I carefully choose books to educate me in a variety of areas, including business, family, mindfulness, and health. When I complete my walk each day, I feel energized and inspired, ready to face challenges and make the world a better place.

While a long walk, rain or shine, might not be for everyone, it is one way to get moving. Walking is an easy and inexpensive way to begin being active. But is walking enough to help you get the level of exercise you need? According to a 2018 study from the American Heart Association (AHA), it is.

Many people wonder whether a more intense workout is better for you than a low-impact activity such as walking. The research from the AHA revealed that any type of movement can have significant benefits for your body. The study used survey data on physical activity and death rates from nearly 5,000 American adults, looking at their total minutes of overall daily activity as well as their total minutes of intense or concentrated daily activity.

The former category included walking and completing tasks throughout the day, whereas the latter included workouts such as cycling classes, interval training, and marathon training, where the exercise spell lasted at least five minutes at a time. The study found that people who did at least thirty minutes a day of either moderate or vigorous exercise were less likely to die from any health cause than people who did no daily activity.

Even a moderate amount of movement can significantly improve your health. That's good news for those of us who don't want to sweat it out for hours at the gym or aren't about to train for a marathon or triathlon. Not to say those things aren't beneficial—if you want to do them. Remember, the key to incorporating exercise into your routine is to find something sustainable and enjoyable, rather than forcing yourself to exercise in ways you find uncomfortable.

What kinds of exercise might you choose? The key, as the research above indicates, is to start with any movement you enjoy. In D.I.E.T., the *E* is for *enjoy being active*.

If you are interested in digging a little deeper into physical fitness, consider incorporating the four most important exercises, as identified by Harvard Health Publishing, into your routine. Of course, discuss any change in exercise with your doctor first.

1. Aerobic Exercise

This type of movement gets your blood pumping and will increase your heart rate. Regular aerobic exercise, including brisk walking, can improve heart and lung health, lower blood pressure, burn body fat, reduce inflammation, and provide other benefits. Regular aerobic exercise can also reduce the risks of heart disease, stroke, type 2 diabetes, certain types of cancer, and mood disorders such as depression.

Walking, running, jogging, cycling, and dancing are all examples of aerobic exercises. If you're so inclined, you can also bring out the spandex and leg warmers and fire up a step aerobics video.

2. Strength Training

Because we lose muscle mass as we age, strength training plays an important part in staying healthy. This type of exercise can help you have an easier time with everyday tasks such as lifting heavy objects, standing up from a chair, and walking up a flight of stairs. Strength exercises help stimulate bone growth, lower blood sugar, and improve balance and posture. They also contribute to weight loss and can reduce stress on your joints.

Strength training doesn't just mean lifting weights. Body weight exercises such as push-ups, squats, and lunges can also help you build and retain muscle mass. Best of all, they require no expensive equipment and are easy to do at home.

3. Stretching

Just as strength training helps improve your muscle mass, stretching helps those muscles function properly. When you neglect to add stretching to your exercise routines, you put yourself at risk for muscle cramps, pain, damage, and strains.

Exercises such as yoga and Pilates provide excellent opportunities to improve your flexibility. However, you don't have to do these as stand-alone workouts. Stretching can help you warm up before an aerobic workout so you avoid painful muscle strains and tears.

4. **Balance Exercises**

Our vision, inner ear, leg muscles, and joints all break down as we age. Improving your balance can help you strengthen these systems. This, in turn, will help you avoid slips, trips, and falls. Yoga and tai chi are good exercises to do if you want to focus on your balance.

If you are thinking about adding a different type of exercise to your routine, consider hiring a trainer or coach to help you get started. We hire experts to help us meet our business goals, create marketing campaigns, manage our retirement income, and remodel our homes, but we often fail to invest in the same way in achieving our fitness goals.

The Critical Message: Do What You Enjoy

I want to repeat that the key here is to think of exercise as activity you enjoy. One of the best ways to stick to your fitness goals is to find something you actually like doing. If walking multiple miles on a treadmill sounds like torture to you, do something different. Experiment until you find what you enjoy. You're more likely to stick with the activity over the long run if you take this approach.

I've kept walking because I found that it was an excellent source of stress relief. Years ago I discovered that taking even a short walk on my lunch break got me out of the corporate office and left me feeling better than I had at the end of the morning.

I listen to an audiobook as I'm walking outside or on the elliptical at home. This helps me add education and professional development to my workouts—another way to keep my mind sharp, and I love the exercise I'm getting. I'll go into detail in the next chapter about how important thinking is in D.I.E.T. For now, it's enough to say that thinking correctly is at the core of health. Feeding your brain is essential.

Listening and learning while I walk is a joy to me, but walking isn't the only activity I enjoy. Jogging, hiking, yoga, dancing, and even bowling all get me up and energized. And I haven't done it yet, but I really want to try wall climbing. I've recently turned sixty years old, and I'm excited by the idea of a new challenge. It's never too late to try something new!

I love these simple words of advice from Tom Rath: "How much should you exercise? The scientific answers to this question often conflict with one another based on the type of exercise or whether the study targeted heart disease, weight loss, or a different outcome. Yet there is a simple answer for most of us: a little more than you are exercising today."

Exercise for Mood and Memory

In an article called "There's Even More Evidence That One Type of Exercise Is the Closest Thing to a Miracle Drug That We Have," Erin Brodwin asks, "Do you want an all-natural way to lift your mood, improve your memory, and protect your brain against age-related cognitive decline?" If you answer, yes, start building thirty to forty minutes of aerobic exercise into your schedule two to four times each week.

Brodwin points to multiple studies that provide evidence that regular aerobic exercise (any movement that raises your heart rate and gets you sweating) may improve the health of your brain and slow down the aging process.

Even healthy older adults find that the normal aging process affects memory, bringing mild cognitive decline. For some, but not all, this decline is a precursor to Alzheimer's. Regular aerobic exercise seems to defend against some of this decline.

The mechanism behind this protective effect is still a mystery, but it might be that exercise strengthens important pathways in the brain.

For example, one study involving older adults showed that walking for thirty minutes a day for twelve weeks strengthened connectivity in a region of the brain where weakened connections have been linked to memory loss.

Another study, involving only older women, found that aerobic exercise was tied to an increase in the size of the hippocampus, an area of the brain involved in learning and memory. While more studies are needed, the results of these and other studies are promising.

If preventing cognitive decline isn't enough to motivate us to exercise, the boost it provides to our mental health could be.

An article from Harvard Health Publishing reminds us of a simple truth: exercise is a form of physical stress. So how does stressing the body leave us feeling relaxed and in a better mood? How does the widely reported runner's high work? The article offers the following explanation:

> *The mental benefits of aerobic exercise have a neurochemical basis. Exercise reduces levels of the body's stress hormones, such as adrenaline and cortisol. It also stimulates the production of endorphins, chemicals in the brain that are the body's natural painkillers and mood elevators.*
>
> *Behavioral factors also contribute to the emotional benefits of exercise. As your waistline shrinks and your strength and stamina increase, your self-image will improve. You'll earn a sense of mastery and control, of pride and self-confidence. Your renewed vigor and energy will help you succeed in many tasks, and the discipline of regular exercise will help you achieve other important lifestyle goals.*

In addition to these benefits, exercise provides time to take a break or get away from the constant pressures of life. Whether you are working on a demanding project at the office or trying to juggle the constant barrage of life's demands, time spent exercising can break the stress cycle and provide a type of reset to your body and mind.

Learn more at:

Erin Brodwin, "There's Even More Evidence that One Type of Exercise is the Closest Thing to a Miracle Drug that We Have." BusinessInsider.com.

"Exercising to Relax," HealthHarvard.edu.

chapter nine

Tending Your Mental Garden: Think

If there are such things as brain exercise, brain movement, and brain therapy, I believe I experience it through the audiobooks I listen to as take my daily walks. I started listening to books on entrepreneurship with the goal of becoming a better businessperson. Then someone recommended an author, and I gave that author a try. I made wonderful discoveries this way. For example, I remember the first time I read a book by Brian Tracy and simply loved it.

Tracy's books, including *Believe It to Achieve It*, co-written with Christina Stein, PhD, empower while they educate. They are thought-focused as well as practical, including insights on how to regulate and focus our thoughts for success. For example, Tracy will tell you in a minute: if you think you're not going to be successful, you're not going to be successful.

I've come to realize that while thinking may come last in my D.I.E.T. acronym, it also belongs at the beginning. If you can't regulate your mind and flood it with healthy thoughts, all you have is discipline. Sheer discipline is rarely enough to keep focus, energy, and internal motivation high enough to sustain practices that lead to achieving your goals. You may have small successes, but you won't have that hard-to-define thing we know as well-being.

Over time, my "diet" of audiobooks helped me to shift my mindset. I began envisioning myself moving forward and started making changes in that direction. It wasn't long until those changes began showing up in my productivity.

My practice of listening to audiobooks while I walk fills my mind with positive thoughts. Audiobooks work for me, but there are countless other ways to motivate and educate yourself. Options include TED talks, podcasts, webinars, conferences, books, and mastermind groups.

I try to reflect on a motivational or inspirational thought every day. For example, at the beginning of each year, I choose a calendar or book with affirmations to work through. Whether I review this item in the morning or evening, it feeds my spirit throughout the year.

In addition to calendars and books, I use social media. I have several great apps on my phone that conveniently deliver affirmations and motivational thoughts. These are all reminders to focus my thoughts positively and productively.

I'm deeply grateful to also have a network of women on whom I can call when I feel low. When COVID-19 shook the foundations of my business, my network of supportive friends made a huge difference. I would text a couple of friends and write *Hey, I'm really discouraged; let's jump on the line.* By the time we finished the call, we were all lifted because we had fed our brains in a healthy way.

Think of Your Brain As a Garden

The first step in regulating your thinking is awareness of the thoughts you have. Rick Hanson, PhD, psychologist, and senior fellow of the Greater Good Science Center at University of California, Berkeley, reminds us that we have great influence on who we become. While genetics are important, they don't have the power to lock us into any state. We have the ability to determine our way forward in life, the capacity to write our own stories. In short, we can change for the better. We might not be able to become rocket scientists or best-selling novelists, but we can be better tomorrow than we are today.

Positive change is linked to attention and learning. Dr. Hanson says, "Your nervous system is designed to be changed by your experiences—the technical term for this is experience-dependent neuroplasticity. Your experiences depend on what you're paying attention to."

It's not necessarily easy to control attention. Our thoughts can run wild with our endless list of tasks, worries about the kids, concerns about bills, frustrations with colleagues, and caregiving responsibilities. We are often *thoughtless* about the directions of *our thoughts*—or at least about our ability to control them. This is where mindfulness, which is essentially exercise for the attention muscle, comes in.

Mindfulness is the practice of staying in the present and noticing what's going on in your thoughts, your body, and your surroundings. Those who engage in regular practice of mindfulness report feeling calmer and more grounded than those who don't. Many scientific studies have confirmed the connection between the practice of mindfulness and positive biological outcomes.

What do you do when, through mindfulness exercises or simple observation, you notice that your thoughts, moods, or physical sensations are mostly negative and stressful? Dr. Hanson suggests a perspective and provides practical tools to help. The following material is adapted from his book (with Forrest Hanson) called *Resilient: How to Grow an Unshakable Core of Calm, Strength, and Happiness.*

Begin by thinking about your thinking. "Imagine that your mind is a garden," Dr. Hanson writes. "You can tend to it in three ways: observe it, pull weeds, and plant flowers."

Observing your garden means simply noticing what's there—without judgment. This process is fundamental to understanding what is happening inside you and what might be driving you. Being present to yourself, your sensations, your emotions, and your desires is fundamental to change. In an observation, however, you aren't trying to change what's there. You are just observing it and sitting with it.

Pulling weeds in your mental garden is a more active step. It involves decreasing the negative, painful, or harmful by "preventing, reducing, or ending it." You might practice a relaxation exercise, vent your frustration to a friend, or distract yourself from self-critical thoughts by watching a movie or playing a game. Also be careful not to inadvertently plant weeds in your own mental garden. Are you paying too much attention to social media, grumbling about things you can't control, or watching violent television shows? Notice which activities plant weeds in your mind and pull those activities out of your life.

Planting flowers is also an active step. It involves intentionally adding positive things to your life. These might include scheduling a massage, spending time with friends, remembering a wonderful vacation, or reaching out to help someone in need.

While any one of these methods—observing, planting, or weeding—can dramatically improve your thinking, all three are crucial in fully tending to the garden of your mind.

Observing and nurturing your mental garden is an exercise in ensuring that your needs as a human being are met. This is essential to effective self-care.

Observing Your Garden: Prioritizing Needs

In preparing to write this book, I had an aha moment when talking with Dr. Shanequa Fleming. She said, "The beliefs we have equate to the decisions we make. And those decisions are indicative of our thoughts, our feelings, and our actions. The results we get stem from our beliefs."

One belief that undermines the success and happiness of many women is the belief that their needs either come last or don't belong in the picture at all. This was the belief behind many of my choices when I was a young wife, mother, graduate student, and emerging entrepreneur.

I wish that during that time in my life I had heard and taken these words of Dr. Rick Hanson to heart:

A healthy body and mind do not come from denying, 'overcoming,' or transcending needs. They are instead the natural result of taking care of your needs, and being mindful of the needs of others. It's the needs we push away that are often the most important to embrace.

Sometimes we genuinely need to say no to an assignment or opportunity and take a soak in a bathtub or a get couple of hours away from our kids or office. Realizing, accepting, and acting on this reality is a path to well-being and productivity. This is self-care, and it's how we love ourselves and get the energy to care for others and manage our many responsibilities.

Michelle, Emebo, MPH, CCRP, provides a great example. At a routine appointment in her third trimester of pregnancy, Emebo learned that her blood pressure was suddenly very high. Throughout the first two trimesters, her blood pressure had been normal, but now it was a big concern. During the five weeks leading up to delivery, Emebo went to the clinic each week, hoping her blood pressure had returned to normal. It had not.

Against expectations, neither Emebo's blood pressure nor weight returned to normal after the birth of her daughter. Emebo also experienced four months of postpartum depression. To add to the stress, when returning to work after maternity leave, Emebo went into a new, more responsible role as clinical research manager.

At the advice of her medical providers, Emebo began taking blood pressure medication and entered therapy for her postpartum depression. A year and a half later, she was feeling better, but her blood pressure was still high enough to be a concern. She was also still carrying roughly thirty-five of the fifty pounds she had gained during pregnancy.

When her doctor wanted to increase the dose of her blood pressure medication, Emebo countered. "Before you increase the dose, I want to try to adjust my nutrition and use exercise to lower my blood pressure." The doctor agreed.

Emebo knew that to be healthy over the long term, she would need to make lifestyle changes. She consulted a nutritionist and began and working out at a gym near her home. Ultimately, it took two and one-half years of good nutrition and exercise for Emebo to drop seventy-five pounds and get her blood pressure to a healthy point. Today, Emebo shares her story as a Real Woman volunteer spokesperson for the American Heart Association's Go Red for Women campaign. She reminds us that hypertension and heart disease are real threats for women, especially for African American women. According to a 2019 statistical update by the American Heart Association, 50 percent of African American women have hypertension. The threat isn't just for elderly women; Emebo was thirty years old when first diagnosed.

In our interview for this book, Emebo said:

I made it my personal mantra that I am responsible to take care of myself. I can't be a good mom, a good wife, or an effective manager at work if I'm not taking care of myself. That was my big commitment. I started to cut out the stuff that didn't support my mantra, that broke into the time I needed for meal preparation and exercise.

For example, I gave up some volunteer activities, including some student recruiting for my alma mater, Spelman College. I didn't necessarily give this up forever; I just need to allow my mantra about self-care to determine how I spend time.

I even cut my hair, which was a huge change for me. Before I had my daughter, I had time to get my hair done at the salon. I no longer had that time. I still get my hair done, but the visits are much shorter now.

The more I figured out how to prioritize in my personal life, the more I understood that prioritizing is a transferable skill. We think so many of the things that come into our lives are important, but they simply are not.

Emebo learned to give herself grace as she was making her lifestyle changes, and she learned how to give that same grace to her coworkers, colleagues, and team members. She said:

I began to focus more on how I could help my team get better than on who had made a mistake and needed to be corrected.

We examined practices at work and cut things that were busy work, things we did because we had always done them. We also added practices, such as fifteen-minute mindfulness breaks, to allow people to reset and be in the right frame of mind to work with patients.

◇◇◇◇◇◇◇◇◇◇

You may have seen the Healthy Eating Plate, developed by the Harvard T.H. Chan School of Public Health, which is an update from the food pyramid that was the accepted nutritional guide during my childhood. The updated nutritional guide depicts a plate signifying one meal, divided as follows: ¼ grain, ¼ protein, ½ fruits and vegetables (with vegetables slightly more than ¼ and fruits slightly less than ¼). These categories, in these proportions, constitute a healthy nutritional diet—as least from a high-view perspective.

Researchers David Rock, PhD, executive director of the NeuroLeadership Institute, and Daniel Siegel, MD, executive director of the Mindsight Institute and clinical professor at the David Geffen School of Medicine at the University of California, Los Angeles, asked themselves what might be on a plate depicting daily activities (nutrients) for a healthy mind. The resulting Healthy Mind Platter recommends seven essential mental activities. In the debate on work-life balance, this is a fresh perspective—one that makes a lot of sense. For me, it was an eye-opener.

As you consider the following "nutrients," remember these are recommended foods for the mind. According to the Healthy Mind Platter, we need servings of each on a regular basis. In an ideal world, we'd serve ourselves a bit of each every day.

Focus Time. This is time spent focusing on goal-oriented tasks and challenges. Examples include finishing a project for work, completing a home improvement, and preparing a fancy meal.

Play Time. We play when we allow ourselves to be spontaneous or creative. The options for play are as unique as the individual. Examples include working on an art project, playing Frisbee, and baking the perfect pie.

Connecting Time. We enrich our minds when we connect with people, nature, and experiences. Examples include sharing coffee with a friend, hosting a dinner party, and taking a solitary walk in the woods.

Physical Time. Moving our bodies is medicine for body *and* mind. Examples include going for a walk, playing with our kids or pets outside, and hitting the gym.

Time In. In our activity-crazed culture, we often fail to take time to reflect on our thoughts, feelings, and decisions. Journaling, meditating, and writing a gratitude list are examples of time in.

Down Time. Slowing things down to let our minds relax and wander is a necessary nutrient for the mind. Examples include watching a movie, reading a book, and sitting quietly on a patio.

Sleep Time. Mind and body both need to recover from busy, stressful days. Research shows that sleep, which we will explore more deeply in the next chapter, is essential to health and productivity. Michael Breus, PhD, known as the Sleep Doctor, says that the average person needs seven and a half hours of sleep each night. Unfortunately, if you lose sleep while rushing to complete a project, you can't make it up on the weekend.

Obviously, we can't slice and dice our days to fit in every mental nutrient every day, certainly not in equal portions. The goal is to be aware of what we need and structure our lives to meet those needs as best we can.

We know that too much focus time spent working will result in burnout and exhaustion. We might not realize that too much time in (think binge-watching a television series) and not enough connecting time may leave us disconnected from the rest of the world. And, of course, we need appropriate amounts of physical activity and sleep in order to stay healthy mentally and physically.

If you're having trouble determining what's on your metaphorical plate, consider using an app or day planner to track your time. This can help you observe how you're spending your time as well as where you're investing your energy during the day.

Pulling Weeds: Avoiding the Negativity Bias

I like Dr. Hanson's metaphor of pulling the weeds in our mind's garden. Unfortunately, this is easier said than done. Did you know that the human brain is wired to look for the bad in situations? It's a phenomenon known as negativity bias, a survival strategy inherited from our ancestors.

If our prehistoric ancestors missed an opportunity because they weren't paying attention, another opportunity would likely come their way. If they missed a threat from a predator because they weren't paying attention, the game was over. As a result, we are biologically wired to be vigilant about things we perceive as threats. We encode and remember negative events vividly and are on the lookout for similar events.

As Dr. Hanson notes, "The brain is tilted toward survival but against long-term health and well-being." As we continually scan for all the bad in our world, we lose sight of the big picture and everything that's going right. This is how we get stuck in a loop of negativity that makes it harder and harder to spot the positives present in our lives.

To recognize negativity bias in yourself, think about a time when something went wrong. Perhaps this was a mistake that you made at work, a minor argument with a friend, or a criticism you received from a boss or a client. If you are like most people, you recounted the situation in detail, thought of belated responses, and considered what you could have done differently. You might have felt guilty or ashamed, even though the situation didn't warrant that.

According to Dr. Hanson, if nine out of ten things that happen in a day are positive, we are likely to think about and remember the negative one. Again, zeroing in on the trouble was vital to our prehistoric ancestors' survival. But today it's a hindrance rather than a help.

So how do we defeat these negative patterns? The answer comes back to observing and reflecting on our thoughts. Are we unproductively dwelling on a failure, criticism, or negative body image? Can we do something to turn that thought around?

Self-help author Byron Katie developed four questions that can help us keep negative and stressful thoughts under control. The first step is writing the thought down. Maybe the thought is chronic, such as *I'm not a success* or *I'll never be healthy*, or maybe the negative thought is tied to a particular situation. Once you have written your negative thought down, ask yourself four questions about this particular thought:

1. **Is it true?** Think of the situation as objectively as possible. Is there actual evidence that your negative thought is grounded in reality?

2. **Can you absolutely know it's true?** Your gut instinct may have told you that you are stuck in a negative reality. But how are you measuring this as fact? Again, dig deep to investigate this thought and poke holes in your own logic.

3. **How do you react—what happens—when you believe that thought?** Does it actually feel good to hold on to a negative thought? What sensations come up in your body? If agonizing over the success of your business or career makes you feel sick to your stomach or gives you a headache, you know it's time to change this belief. Write these feelings down and be specific.

4. **Who would you be without the thought?** Imagine the possibility of letting go of this thought for good. How would you feel without

it? Empowered? Proud? Focused on your successes? Take time to visualize a future where the opposite of the negativity is true for you.

Working through Katie's method provides the opportunity to turn your negative thought around. Once you know that a statement like *I can never be healthy* isn't actually true, you can replace it with a better thought. You might choose an affirmation: *I am taking consistent steps toward better health*, or *Every day I am getting stronger and healthier*, or *I love my body just as it is*.

By observing and "pulling" your negative thoughts, you can better prime yourself to see possibilities. By recognizing what's working, you can strengthen the neural pathways that pick up on positivity. Remember, your brain is designed for experience-dependent neuroplasticity. You determine what's happening in your brain by your muscle of attention.

Planting Flowers: Getting to the Good Stuff

Pulling weeds and removing our negative biases is one thing. Planting flowers is another. Dr. Hanson encourages us to "see the jewels around you" and create some of our own.

You create a jewel when you give or accept a kindness, intentionally relax with a cup of coffee, or be fully present to a sunset. You also create a jewel when you undertake a task that requires effort and rewards you with a sense of satisfaction.

I once saw a greeting card that read *Hope and fear cannot occupy the same space. Invite one to stay.* I've also heard that it's impossible to concentrate on your breath and a negative thought at the same time.

Motivational speakers, psychologists, and successful entrepreneurs all talk about gratitude as a mindset—flowers we have the ability to plant. Examples of gratitude practices include listing five things you are grateful each night, keeping a gratitude journal, and asking each member of the family to name one good thing about the day over dinner. While these are great exercises, gratitude becomes life-changing only when it becomes a mindset.

Gratitude, which helps you focus on what you have rather than what you don't have, is one practice to develop a positive mindset. Another is to step back and examine events from a big-picture or long-view perspective. For example, I try not to let something such as a fender bender ruin my day. Any accident with a car has the potential to be tragic. A fender bender is inconvenient and may be expensive, but it's far from tragic. Daily frustrations that come with colleagues and kids are easier to manage when looked at from a big-picture vantage.

It's also important to keep my frustrations with myself in perspective. I learned from Dr. Michelle Robin that I don't have to consider any day a failure. I plant a flower in my mental garden by accepting that it's unrealistic to expect perfection of myself or anyone else. I can think of my days as A days, B days, and C days. On a C day, I can wallow in disappointment or simply take a deep breath and prepare for an A day tomorrow. I can remind myself of the many wonderful things in my life, regardless of a single day's performance. For instance, my mother is safe, my daughter is happy, and I have my health.

You can plant flowers in your mental garden by developing mutually supportive relationships. Having the right people around you—even virtually—can help boost your mood and gain perspective on bad days. Give yourself permission to weed out people who are toxic in your life—you have that right. If it's not feasible to completely break contact with a negative person, set boundaries and stick to them.

When your positive support network isn't readily available, turn to other resources to change your thoughts and focus on the positives. Read an inspiring book, watch a motivational TED talk, or choose affirmations to repeat to yourself.

You can also revisit the Healthy Mind Platter as a guide for how you can plant some "mind flowers" in your daily life. Check in with how you're feeling and choose an appropriate mental nutrient for that day.

Craving adventure? Go for a hike or visit a new business.
Need connection? Call a friend or invite someone over for lunch.
Want time to yourself? Read a book, take a walk, or try a restorative yoga practice.

Low on energy? Meditate, soak in the tub, or take a nap.
Low mood? Perform a service for someone in need.

Planting flowers in your mind isn't the same as ignoring realities. We know that our brains focus disproportionately on the bad, and that this practice doesn't serve us well. Planting flowers is countering this reality by noticing and creating the good that coexists with the struggles. It's gaining perspective and increasing your resilience to face whatever life brings your way. Pay attention to your garden. Remember, this is self-care, not self-indulgence.

Is Positive Thinking Enough?

A healthy mind isn't a matter of seeing the world through rose-colored glasses or expecting to attract good things by positive thoughts alone. According to Richard Citrin, PhD, and Alan Weiss, PhD, authors of *The Resilience Advantage*, we need to blend aspiration with action if we want our lives to move in a positive direction.

Citrin and Weiss point to an experiment conducted by NYU psychology professor Gabrielle Oettingen, who asked two groups of students to visualize their upcoming week. One group was told to fantasize only about good things: "great parties, good grades, good health, and so on." The other group was told to think about neutral situations in their upcoming week, just whatever was on their schedule.

Who had the better week? In terms of productivity, the neutral group accomplished more. It appears that the positive-only fantasies may have made students complacent.

The winning strategy to achieve any goal is to visualize your goal as complete, then act to move it in that direction. The winning strategy also includes anticipating problems that could arise and planning for the best possible outcomes.

Oettingen developed a methodology for this type of goal setting called WOOP, which stands for *wish, outcome, obstacles,* and *plan*. The process is as follows:

Wish. Decide what you want to achieve. This goal can pertain to your personal or professional life. It should be something challenging and quantifiable that you can accomplish within a specific timeframe. (Think SMART goals here: *specific, measurable, attainable, relevant*, and *time-based*.)

Outcome. Next, picture the outcome of this goal. What is it that you genuinely want? For instance, if you want a new client for your business, you might picture the outcome as a testimonial from a happy customer, another project for your portfolio, or a big check as your reward. Reach for the best possible outcome so you have an idea of what's at stake.

Obstacles. Identify what is standing in the way of your success. Although none of us like to think about the difficulties in our journey, it's best to plan for them if—or when—they occur. Visualize what could go wrong, but don't fret!

Plan. Once you have an idea of the potential roadblocks on the path to your goal, generate a plan to prevent or mitigate these roadblocks. Create your plan for success. For example, if you have a goal to lose weight, your obstacle may be that on busy days you habitually reach for a quick snack in the vending machine. If you know this is a potential issue, set aside time to prepare healthy snacks you can grab and go before you leave home.

Citrin and Weiss add a fifth factor to WOOP: **Behaviors.** Identify behaviors that will help your plan succeed. Be specific as you list these so that you have a plan of action in case the obstacles you've visualized occur.

For example, if your goal is to secure a new client, one behavior might be making the initial phone call or following up on a prospect's email in a timely manner. If your goal is to lose weight, the first behavior might be scheduling a couple of hours on the weekend to prepare healthy meals for the week ahead. Keeping your vision of a successful future in mind will help you stick to your positive behaviors.

However, positive thinking alone won't get you where you want to go. This doesn't mean that positive thinking isn't worthwhile. Citrin and Weiss describe two approaches to positive thinking that can change your life.

1. Think more positively and follow it up with action.
2. Adopt positive behaviors and, with some success, you'll see a natural change occur in your thinking.

Oettingen's WOOP process helps you use both methods to take realistic steps toward achieving your goals.

Learn more in Richard Citrin and Alan Weiss. *The Resilience Advantage: Stop Managing Stress and Find Your Resilience.*

chapter ten

Refresh and Restore: Sleep

I can't recall a single conversation I've had with a doctor in which the doctor talked about the link between sleep and how it directly affects a person's physical and mental health. Given that I have never missed an annual physical, that's saying something. Doctors have asked how I'm sleeping, how I'm eating, and how much I'm exercising. Perhaps the conversations never went any further because I always answered that I was sleeping well.

It wasn't until I started educating myself about how to be a healthier person that I noticed experts talking about how critical our sleep habits are to our well-being—or our lack thereof. Our sleep affects all the things for which we seek medical attention: stress, anxiety, excess weight, and various diseases. That's why this chapter is devoted to sleep.

I've always considered myself a good sleeper. I have a consistent history of working hard and being tired at night. No matter how stressful a day is, I'm asleep as soon as my head hits the pillow. The only exception is when I'm worried about a family member. In that case, I wake up in the middle of the night with my concerns. I'm not sure even the best sleep habits can be effective when I'm worried about my mother or daughter. At the same time, I've learned that a lot about how I sleep is within my control.

It turns out that sleep is not equal. Getting the recommended hours of sleep is one thing; getting high-quality sleep is another. Even though I have no problem falling asleep, I have not historically had the healthiest sleep patterns. I can't pinpoint how poor sleep quality has negatively affected my health, energy, and productivity over the years, but research says it has.

One of my less-than-healthy habits is the tendency to fall asleep with the television on. Experts agree that the blue light from television and other electronics inhibits sleep. Blue light confuses the natural sleep signals of your body. You improve the quality of your sleep when you shut off electronics a couple of hours before bed and remove the portable ones from the bedroom.

I was surprised to learn that you can't make up for sleep you lose. I used to sometimes sleep late on Saturday or Sunday, especially after a big week, thinking I was doing myself a favor. I'd wake up feeling worse and wonder, Why do I feel so sluggish when I got extra sleep? Now I understand that I'm doing my body a favor when I stick to a consistent sleep pattern: weekdays and weeknights the same.

On the bright side, I've discovered that my grandmother instilled in me some healthy habits about relaxing and preparing myself for sleep. I remember peeking in the door to my grandmother's bedroom and seeing a spotless room with pure white furniture and bedding. That room looked like heaven on earth. If I had a vision of heaven as a child, it was my grandmother's bedroom. While I loved to peek in, I would not cross the doorway into that room because it was strictly off limits to children.

Today I understand that Grandmother's bedroom was her sanctuary, not a place for entertainment and play. It was a place where she had her private moments with God in prayer and where she lay down to rest at night.

My memories of that room and the feelings I had as I looked into it are vivid. I've followed in Grandmother's footsteps in making my bedroom a personal and beautiful sanctuary. If I had a significant other, of course, the bedroom would be for us both. I'm single, so I rarely allow anyone in that space. It's a very personal space, and I protect it.

The calming ambiance of my bedroom sets the stage for sleep. Other practices that help me slow down and prepare for sleep include hot baths and lovely scents, especially lavender. Enjoying such things before bed isn't indulgence, it's self-care.

◇◇◇◇◇◇◇◇◇

One day in 2007, while sitting at her desk answering emails and talking on the phone, columnist/businesswoman Arianna Huffington fainted. She woke up in a pool of blood with a broken cheekbone and a cut over her eye that required five stitches. Imagine how scary that was.

After weeks of medical tests, Huffington was diagnosed with exhaustion. While the diagnosis must have seemed anticlimactic, it resulted from months of working eighteen-hour days building the Huffington Post website. It's in the ugly category of "who can you blame but yourself?"

In her TED talk, Huffington describes her journey of rediscovering the value of sleep. After studying and meeting with multiple medical doctors and scientists, she says, "I'm here to tell you that the way to a more productive, more inspired, more joyful life is getting enough sleep."

Huffington has become a sleep evangelist who says her collapse was a wakeup call that changed her life. She is sought out regularly by media outlets to share her expertise on sleep. Ten years after her collapse, Huffington published *The Sleep Revolution: Transforming Your Life One Night at a Time*.

In a 2018 interview with John Dickerson on CBS, Huffington reported that a long-ingrained perspective among professionals is that tiredness is a sign of productivity is changing. Some top-tier executives are speaking out about their intentional practice of getting enough sleep. Still, Huffington claims that our addiction to technology, along with the drive to accomplish more, causes many to have problems getting enough sleep.

In the interview, Huffington pointed to tips to improving sleep that were published on her website, thriveglobal.com. A key piece of advice is not to sleep with your phone. If you resist this suggestion, chances are you are among the 70 percent of people who sleep with their phones.

The tip is to pick a time at the end of each day to turn off your phone and remove it from your bedroom. Huffington stresses, "It's not just the blue light; it's the fact that our phones are depositories of every problem, of every project, and you need to disconnect from that to be able to fall under."

In addition to sleeping with their phones, most people also check their phones "before they take their first truly conscious breath." This goes against all that neuroscience tells us about taking time each day to set an intention as soon as we wake up. When you check your phone first thing in the morning, you begin your day with a reactive rather than a proactive stance.

Huffington encourages us to stop with our endless excuses about why we have to be so connected to our phones. And don't tell her you need your phone for an alarm clock. She will tell you that you can buy a beautiful alarm clock from Pottery Barn for thirty-five dollars.

Huffington's story serves as a dramatic cautionary tale: If you don't sleep, you can't function. It turns out you are also likely to be overweight, even obese. Dr. Jason Fung points to population studies that consistently link limited sleep with excess weight. These studies show that sleeping five to six hours a night is associated with more than a 50 percent increased risk of weight gain. The fewer hours of sleep, the more weight gain. Dr. Fung reports:

> *Sleep deprivation is a potent psychological stressor and thus stimulates cortisol. This, in turn, results in both high insulin levels and insulin resistance. A single night of sleep deprivation increases cortisol levels by more than 100 percent. By the next evening, cortisol is still 37 to 40 percent higher . . .*
>
> *Both leptin and ghrelin, key hormones in the control of body fatness and appetite, show a daily rhythm and are disrupted by sleep disturbance . . . It's not the sleep loss per se that is harmful, but the activation of the stress hormones and hunger mechanisms. Getting enough good sleep is essential to any weight loss plan.*

<><><><><><><>

When it comes to explaining the science behind sleep, Michael Breus, PhD, known as the Sleep Doctor, is a leading expert and resource. Dr. Breus has been called upon by Oprah, *The New York Times*, *The Wall Street*

Journal, Dr. Oz, *The Early Show*, SiriusXM, and more to share advice and explain the science of sleep. I had the privilege of interviewing Dr. Breus for Wellness Wednesday, one of the weekly webinars hosted by Woman Diverse Media during the pandemic. The material that follows is adapted from this program. A brief overview of science sets the context for recommendations. Take a deep breath though, working your way through Dr. Breus's science is a bit like drinking from a firehose.

Two distinct systems in the brain help you fall asleep. One is your *sleep drive*, the other is your *sleep rhythm* (circadian rhythm).

Your sleep drive is a lot like hunger. You feel hungry and begin to eat; the hunger subsequently subsides. The same holds true with sleep. Over the course of the day, you get sleepier and sleepier as a substance called adenosine accumulates at a specific receptor site in your brain. You sleep and the feeling of sleepiness subsides.

The second part of the sleep system is your sleep rhythm. When your sleep drive and sleep rhythm systems are in balance, you get good sleep. When they are out of balance, you get either low-quality sleep or develop a disorder such as apnea, narcolepsy, or insomnia.

Each night, you have a number of *sleep cycles*, roughly ninety minutes each, which are broken into *five stages*. You go from wake to stage one, to stage two, down to stage three, four, back to stage two, and into REM sleep. This pattern is considered one sleep cycle. Here is the kicker: you have to go in this order to complete a sleep cycle and benefit from each stage.

Stage one functions like a door that opens to your unconscious; it gets sleep started. Stage two makes up the bulk of sleep—about 50 percent of the night. Stages three and four, together, are known as the beauty sleep, during which the growth hormone is emitted and cellular repair occurs. If you're interested in delaying the effects of aging or losing weight, you want as much stage three and four sleep as you can get. Remember, you have to reach this stage in the cycle to get the benefit.

The final stage is REM—or rapid eye moment—sleep. This is the phase when mental restoration takes place. During REM sleep, you move information from short-term to long-term memory. You might think of the process as your brain organizing information and putting it into a file cabinet. Somehow, your dreams are involved.

The average person has five sleep cycles per night, which equates to seven and a half hours—not the eight hours you've been hearing about for your whole life. The amount of sleep you actually need is personal. As a general guideline, shoot for somewhere between seven and nine hours.

The Sleep Doctor himself goes to bed at midnight and wakes between 6:15 and 6:20 every day. This is possible because the quality of his sleep is extremely high. He says, "By improving your sleep quality, you can shrink your sleep quantity, which is amazing."

One more piece to the science of sleep before we get to Dr. Breus's recommendations: your body has a hard-wired chronotype; it's written in your genes. Even if you haven't heard the term before, you are familiar with the concept. If you've described yourself as an early bird or a night owl, you've been talking about your chronotype. Perhaps you are somewhere in in between those two extremes. For good sleep, it's important to identify and work with your chronotype rather than against it.

You can access my complete interview with Dr. Breus at www.WomanDiversityMedia.com. For now, here's a partial list of the many recommendations he shared on the webinar.

Know your sleep rhythm and sleep drive. You get the best quality sleep when you honor your body's natural patterns, especially by being consistent about when you go to sleep and when you get up. Sleeping late on the weekends just messes up your sleep rhythm and hurts the quality of your sleep.

Know your chronotype. Knowing and working with the body that nature gave you makes sense. To find out about your chronotype, visit chronoquiz.com. You'll learn your chronotype, plus get specific recommendations related to your type, courtesy of Dr. Breus.

Stop drinking caffeine around two p.m. Caffeine is a stimulant with a half-life of between six and eight hours. Shutting off the caffeine at two p.m. gives you eight hours for the caffeine to work its way out of your system before a ten p.m. bedtime. Even if you can drink caffeine later in the day and still fall asleep, there are consequences. Having caffeine in your system reduces the quality of your sleep. Caffeine—and alcohol in particular—affects the quality of sleep stages three and four, your beauty sleep.

Stop eating three to four hours before your bedtime. Human bodies are not designed to digest food lying down. It's that simple and that inescapable.

Limit the number and timing of alcoholic drinks. If you choose to drink, do so with dinner, and limit yourself to three drinks or less. Remain hydrated by drinking a glass of water for every glass of alcohol you drink. The alcohol will leave your system after about three hours.

Take vitamin D as a supplement. During the COVID-19 pandemic, studies revealed that roughly 90 percent of the fatalities occurred in people who were vitamin D deficient. According to Dr. Breus, vitamin D acts like a big circadian pacemaker. He recommends taking vitamin D-3 and magnesium every morning.

Exercise daily—but not before bed. Sleep is recovery. If you don't have anything to recover from, you won't sleep well! Twenty to thirty minutes of exercise a day is enough—but get it in early—at least four hours before your bedtime. Exercise increases core body temperature, which is great. Unfortunately, we need our core body temperature to be lower when it's time to fall asleep.

Limit or block blue light exposure at night. Light from our televisions, computers, and phones send signals that it's time to be awake. Even the banks of lights in our bathrooms can disrupt the natural slowing down that precedes good sleep. Dr. Breus recommends removing your makeup early in the evening to avoid this. You can also purchase blue light blocking glasses.

Schedule an hour before bed for slowing your body down. Begin by turning off your phone. Arianna Huffington would say get that phone out of your bedroom! Dr. Breus recommends using twenty minutes to perform tasks such as preparing for the next day, twenty minutes for personal hygiene, and twenty minutes to meditate or pray, to help yourself slow down to prepare for sleep.

Wake up with water and direct sunlight. Rather than start your day with a jolt of caffeine, take five deep breaths to kick-start your respiratory system. Then drink between fifteen and thirty ounces of room temperature water every morning. Walk over to the window and get some direct sunlight and let your body know it's time to wake up.

I think about the material in this chapter and ask myself, *Who knew?!* In times past, we might have worn our busyness and lack of sleep as a badge of honor. "*Look at me, I'm serious enough about my career to sacrifice. And I love my children enough to sew their Halloween costumes at three a.m.*"

We may still be busy, but now we know that skipping sleep will make matters worse rather than better. When it approaches ten p.m. tonight, I encourage you to lock your phone in a drawer, turn off the lights, and enjoy your sleep.

How You Sleep Tonight Affects How You'll React to Stress Tomorrow

In an article in *Greater Good Magazine*, a publication of the Greater Good Science Center, Elizabeth Hopper, PhD, claims that a good night's sleep makes us more positive and resilient to stress. She describes a study that surveyed nearly two thousand adults over a period of eight days during the pandemic. Each evening participants were asked to report how much they'd slept the night before, whether they had experienced any stressful or positive events, and their overall levels of positive and negative emotions. Results showed that a good night's sleep correlates with higher levels of positive emotions and lower levels of negative ones on the following day. On days that contained a stressful event, participants who had had a good night's sleep reported less of a "hit" to their emotions than those who had not. On days that held positive events, participants who had had a good night's sleep reported a higher boost in positive emotions than those who did not. According to Dr. Hopper, "These benefits were even more pronounced for people who had a greater number of chronic health conditions such as high blood pressure or diabetes."

This research about the impact of sleep on emotions reinforces what we've known all along. Especially during times of high stress, it's critical that we discipline ourselves to engage in good sleep practices. We may not be able to control the influx of pressures that come with life, but we can control whether or not we eat a carton of ice cream while dousing ourselves in the light of our electronics right before bed.

Learn more at Elizabeth Hopper, "Your Sleep Tonight Changes How You React to Stress." GreaterGood.Berkley.edu.

chapter eleven

Tie It Together: Celebrate Results

COVID-19 was a wake-up call for all of us on many levels. For me, it was also an uninvited proving ground. When in-person events were shut down in March 2020, I was roughly a year into my new routines of self-care. I was twenty-plus pounds lighter, eating nutritiously, enjoying my walks, feeding my brain, and engaging in good sleep practices. My energy and sense of well-being was high, and I believed I was functioning at a level of maximum leadership and productivity. I was regularly accomplishing more than I ever had before.

Of course, none of us knew how long the COVID-19 shutdown would last. We only knew that we needed to shift and expand our capacities at home and at work. Those of us in service businesses needed to design high-value experiences and deliver them virtually. Were any of us ready? For me, the answer is yes and no.

I can't explain exactly how it worked, but I'm aware that once I started focusing on taking care of myself, I started taking better care of my business, as well. And as a result, when COVID-19 struck, I was well positioned. In the past, a disruption of such magnitude might have sent me into a depressed mood or made me want to sleep all day.

In 2020, I was physically, mentally, and spiritually ready to address the challenge that came. I had an uptick of stress, as we all did, but I was able to sustain my energy level, attention, and stamina. These are essential ingredients in productivity. I was able to navigate the storm without feeling sluggish or dragged down by the size of the task. I can honestly say that Diversity Woman Media thrived during the pandemic. From where I sit today, the future of my organization is bright.

The first thing that became clear was that my company needed to switch from in-person conferences to virtual ones. We couldn't wait out the shutdown and hope to remain relevant. As you know, I utilized the strong network I had built over the years to research the most innovative, virtual platform available and scheduled our first virtual conferences for August 2020. We held three virtual conferences during the pandemic.

In March, while researching virtual platforms, I sent out motivational messages to our customers, proactively connecting with our community. The responses were positive, affirming the need for us to unite, hold each other up, and share in the challenges of the pandemic together. I could see that my messages were making a difference.

My studies in entrepreneurship had taught me to always listen to my customers. I'll never forget one message I received from a customer and immediately took to heart. It read, *Sheila, your following wants to hear from you. They need you. You need to come up with something innovative.*

If I hadn't had the incentive before, that message would have done the trick. As humans, hearing that we are needed pushes us beyond whatever capacity we believe we have, to reach for something greater. Within thirty days of the first shutdown, my team and I came up with a weekly webinar we named Moving Forward, designed as a resource to help our customers navigate through the challenging times we were all facing.

We had doctors, psychologists, psychiatrists, and business experts all share knowledge and helpful strategies for health and productivity during that period.

The capstone of our Moving Forward webinars was our virtual Power Forward conference, held in November. We kicked off 2021 with a new series of weekly webinars called Wellness Wednesday, which ran until the last Wednesday in March.

The country had started opening up, and the related challenges had shifted. Moving from behind our Zoom cameras brought fresh challenges for our customers, including the fact that many of them found that their clothes had become too tight. Wellness Wednesday webinars dealt with getting back out into the world, including expert insights on nutrition, health, and mental wellness. We capped the Wellness Wednesday series off with a two-day self-care, health, and wellness conference free to the world at the end of April, 2021.

One of the things I am most proud of is developing and registering a national day called World Women's Wellness Day with the National Day Archives. The day, first celebrated on April 20, 2021, will be recognized on the last Friday of every April.

It's a self-affirming and self-check day for women. I encourage you to use World Women's Wellness Day to check the status of your physical and mental health, be that by scheduling a physical, adding an exercise routine, building regular recovery time into your work week, working with a therapist, enrolling in a certification program, or whatever best epitomizes self-care for you. You might even take the weekend to de-stress through spa treatments, mindfulness, or meditation. World Woman's Wellness Day is about you and for you. Celebrate yourself.

◇◇◇◇◇◇◇◇◇◇

As I ready this book for its Fall 2021 publication, the United States is largely open for business, but concerns surrounding COVID-19 are far from over. The future of COVID-19 and its continuing impact on our lives and businesses are unclear.

Of course, COVID-19 is a global pandemic, and none of us are safe until all of us are safe. And even when COVID-19 is under control, experts expect more worldwide pandemics. We have an increased awareness that life is uncertain.

For a long time now, experts have been saying that adaptability and creativity are top-tier leadership skills. If we didn't believe it before, we need to believe it now. While the quest for resilience is not new, it has taken on a new sense of urgency.

As far as this book goes, we have come full circle. The root source of adaptability, creativity, and resilience is self-care. If you are a leader in your workplace, home, extended family, or community, you cannot afford to drain your own tank while taking care of others. You never could afford it, and I hope our time together has made you aware or deepened your conviction about that.

While this book tells my story, I don't intend it to be as much about me as about you. I encourage you to make this book transformational for yourself. Begin by assessing your mindset about self-care. What messages have you heard or absorbed about your right to choose your own path in life? How much of your life is directed at making others feel satisfied or happy? In a theoretical sense, do you believe your needs are as important as the needs of others, including your life partner, kids, bosses, and extended family members? How does that work out in practical terms? How much of your life passion is on hold? If you are struggling against the mindset that self-care for women is selfish, try reaching to your core to discover your own definition of success. Post that definition on your mirror and identify steps to move in that direction.

As a lifelong learner with a doctorate in education, I was shocked to learn that I had never bothered to educate myself about my health until I faced a crisis. In recent years, I've soaked up as much information as I can, and I find myself continually fascinated. Even so, I'll never be, or claim to be, an expert in this area.

I've learned that health, nutrition, and sleep are amazingly complicated, and that everyone's body is unique. Only you can discover the right path for you. That said, this book is full of material from individuals who are experts in their fields. I encourage you to reread the expert material and dig deeper into each area. Use the information at the end of the book to find these professionals and discover how you can learn more from them. And, of course, discuss any changes you plan to make with your own doctor.

For me, the trigger to invest in my own self-care after decades of neglect came from the need to lose weight to avoid disease. I'm still haunted by my cardiologist telling me that my health habits were literally shaving years off my life. Like so many women in our culture, there I was again, on the seemingly impossible quest to lose weight. While my journey began at this dismal spot, I'm grateful that it ended somewhere completely different—with me feeling great and being more productive than I've ever been in my life. It's been liberating to throw out "diet" and embrace D.I.E.T.

As you go forward, I hope you'll remember the acronym that has been so transformational for me. While health and well-being are complicated, this simple acronym has incredible power.

D = drink (Chapter 6): Water is *the* vital nutrient we need to flourish. Many of us are chronically dehydrated, and we often believe we are hungry when we are actually thirsty. Sodas, diet drinks, and alcohol are poor substitutes for water; in fact, many of these beverages increase dehydration as well as pump us full of chemicals. Start each day with a glass of water and keep a bottle on your desk or in your work area for sipping throughout the day.

I = intake (Chapter 7): Everything we put into our systems contributes to our health or lack thereof. We need to take in and enjoy healthy foods, such as vegetables and fruits, and we need to pay attention to additives we inadvertently introduce into our bodies through processed foods. We also need to be aware that we absorb much from our environment, including chemical toxins, criticism, and negativity.

E = exercise (Chapter 8): My life changed when Tom Rath's book *Eat Move Sleep* helped me to redefine exercise as movement I enjoy. If your exercise feels like a burden and drudgery, you have a poor mindset or poor exercise fit—or both. Let's move—let's dance—to our own health!

T = think (Chapter 9): Although thinking comes last in the acronym, it is by far the most important element. Our thoughts drive our reactions and behaviors. We need to intentionally feed our brains with the nutrients of positive, inspiring, motivating, and spiritual messages.

I included a chapter on sleep in this book because good sleep is an essential element of self-care. Dr. Michael Breus's overview of sleep science and his tips for good sleep, found in chapter 10, are amazing. Don't forget Arianna Huffington's compelling argument for removing your phone from your bedroom!

I've been so excited to share what I've learned about personal well-being and productivity through self-care. Whether you are a longtime member of the Diversity Woman Media community, or whether this is your introduction to our organization, you are important to me. Thank you for joining me on this journey toward wellness and productivity. Visit our website, use the resources you find there, attend a conference. I'm cheering for your success and want to hear your stories too.

As I conclude, I issue you a challenge.

The goal of this **twenty-eight-day challenge** is to help you increase your overall self-care through awareness and action.

Your first task is to tear out page 127 and post it in a place where you will see it multiple times a day. Consciously think about the definition of each element each day.

    D – **Drink:** Hydration Is Health
    I – **Intake:** You Are What You Eat and More
    E – **Exercise:** Enjoy How You Move
    T – **Think:** Tend Your Mental Garden

Each day of the week throughout the twenty-eight days (four weeks), you'll be asked to perform an activity that invites you to reflect on that element of D.I.E.T. and take at least a small action related to self-care in that element. Repetition over the four weeks will help you to shift both your thought patterns and behaviors. The small steps required to meet the challenge build upon each other to create a healthy lifestyle you can sustain.

Here is the challenge:

Sundays: Since healthy thinking is the foundation for healthy living, dedicate Sundays to this reflect on T for *Think*. Set yourself up for the week by reviewing the Healthy Mind Platter (https://drdansiegel.com/healthy-mind-platter/), introduced in Chapter 9. Schedule time on your calendar in the coming week for two activities from the platter that you don't typically do. Activities include physical time, focus time, time in, down time, play time, and connect time. Since the platter also lists sleep as an essential component of a healthy mind, commit to good sleep habits throughout the entire week.

Mondays: Increase your awareness of I for *Intake* and strive to increase your intake of vegetables and fruit. Specifically, challenge yourself on Mondays to eat as many colors of the rainbow as possible. Different colors provide you with different nutrients. Experts recommend we strive for five vegetables and fruits a day. Feel free to make one of your servings on Monday a glass of red wine. For a bonus challenge, add an additional serving of a whole grain (oats, whole wheat, quinoa, popcorn, barley, brown rice, wild rice, and couscous) to your intake on Mondays.

Tuesdays: Notice your thoughts (T for *Think*) throughout the day on Tuesdays. Are you spending more time on negative or positive thoughts? Remembering that we inherited a negativity bias from our ancestors, seek to counteract the tendency by practicing gratitude. Consider purchasing a special journal for gratitude at the beginning of the month to use on a daily basis. Each Tuesday, surprise someone with a gratitude message. Make the message more special by sending it via a phone call or card in the mail.

Wednesdays: This is your day to pay special attention to D for *Drink* or hydration. Although the amount of water you need is personal, a general goal of eight glasses of water a day is reasonable. But good hydration habits encompass more than glasses of water. On Wednesdays, try to eat two fruits or vegetables with a high-water content. Examples include lettuce, cucumbers, zucchini, watermelon, and strawberries. Try different herbal teas and/or fruit-infused water. Keep in mind that fruit juices provide hydration—with a load of calories. Drink those sparingly. Also keep in mind that the body is slightly dehydrated after a night's sleep. Be good to yourself: drink a glass water first thing in the morning.

Thursdays: This is another day to increase your awareness of I for *Intake*. Keep a food diary on Thursdays to uncover the amount of healthy and unhealthy foods you take in. Notice how you feel after eating specific foods. Do certain foods make you feel energized and others lethargic? How do specific foods affect your moods? Consider taking a field trip one Thursday to the grocery store to notice the differences in the foods around the perimeter versus those in the central aisles. See what you learn by reading labels on the processed foods in the center aisles. Use another Thursday to explore the Think Dirty website and app (https://thinkdirtyapp.com/), introduced in Chapter 7. Evaluate the safety of your cleaning and beauty products.

Fridays: In the T for *Think* chapter, we learned about Rick Hansen's metaphor as the mind as a garden. He suggests three ways in which we improve the health of our brain: observing our thoughts, pulling weeds (negativity and self-criticism), and planting flowers (engaging in and taking time to appreciate positive thoughts and experiences.) Use Fridays to intentionally plant flowers. Devote twenty minutes on Fridays to appreciate nature, enjoy music, meditate, or pray. For a bonus challenge, identify and celebrate two of your accomplishments from this week.

Saturdays: Think of Saturday as a good day for a little extra sweat. E is for *Exercise* that you *enjoy*. Rather than perform the same old routine at the gym or home space, try something that's new for you on Saturdays. Perhaps you'd like bowling, square dancing, taking a class, riding a bike, or a riding a horse. Maybe a short ride to a park or nature reserve would make a walk or run especially enjoyable. Consider inviting a friend to do something goofy—or rent a child for a game of frisbee.

My reason for writing this book has been to share the knowledge and experience that has transformed my life. I began my journey into well-being to lose weight to stave off the diseases that threatened me due to both heritage and habits. I had no idea that the initiative would transform my entire life, including how I look at myself and the world.

My efforts to educate myself about healthy eating evolved into an education on self-care—and it eventually led me to embrace self-love. The results have been nothing short of transformative. My energy level, my sense of well-being, my relationships with others, and my productivity have skyrocketed. Along the way, I did manage to lose the weight and keep it off.

The twenty-eight-day challenge is a way to solidify what you've learned in this book and push forward your own transformative journey in manageable steps. I don't know the exact steps and practices that will be right for you. You'll have to educate and experiment for yourself, but once you've figured out what works for you, no one will be able to take that away from you. Your well-being and your productivity will soar. So give the twenty-eight day challenge a try—and redefine your own D.I.E.T.

Tear out the following page and use it as your daily reminder of the D.I.E.T. elements. On the back side is a blank calendar for you to use as you wish. Use it to plan your days, track your activity, or a combination of both!

- 🥤 **D – Drink:** Hydration Is Health
- 🍎 **I – Intake:** You Are What You Eat and More
- 👟 **E – Exercise:** Enjoy Being Active
- 🧠 **T – Think:** Tend Your Mental Garden

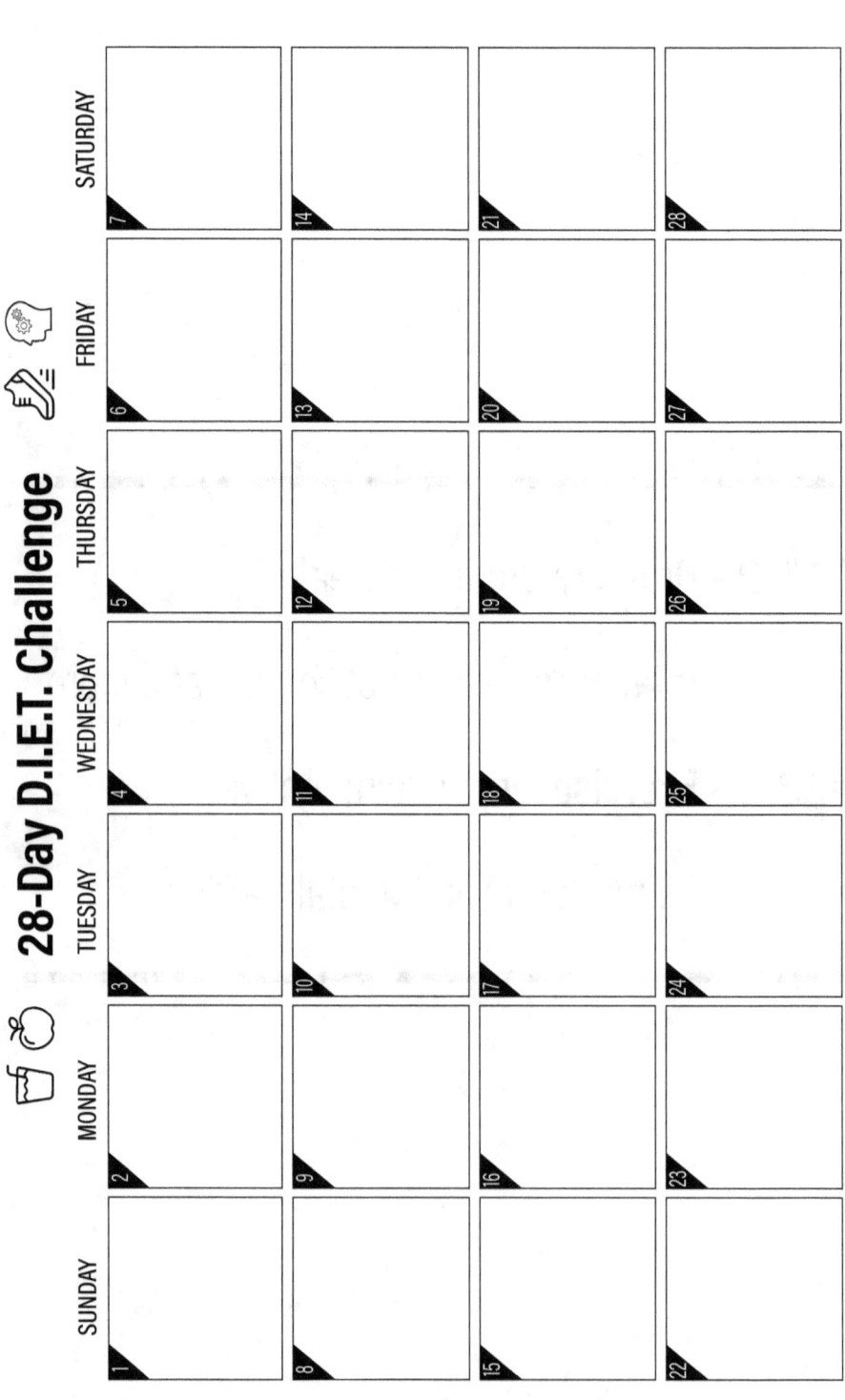

Diversity Woman Media Announces First-ever World Women's Wellness Day,
April 30, 2021

Washington, April 14, 2021 — With more women juggling home, work, caregiving, and a multitude of other new responsibilities as a result of the pandemic, **Diversity Woman Media**, the essential business magazine and community for women professionals and executives, today announced the first-ever **World Women's Wellness Day**. The official health and wellness day for women, sanctioned by National Day Archives, LLC, will be held Friday, April 30, 2021, with future celebrations the last Friday in April. In honor of World Women's Wellness Day, Diversity Woman Media will host its first **free** "Self-care, Health, and Wellness Day," a virtual conference April 29–30 for women all over the world. Register here: https://diversitywoman-selfcare.vfairs.com/en/.

To continue the celebration of wellness, the current issue of *Diversity Woman Magazine*, on newsstands now, is dedicated to self-care and wellness. The digital magazine is available here: https://lsc-pagepro.mydigitalpublication.com/publication/?i=702187.

The official World Women's Wellness Day and free virtual conference initiatives are an extension of Diversity Woman Media's Wellness Wednesday webinars, held during the pandemic to focus on issues, including mental health, managing stress, wellness, self-care, sleep, nutrition, and mindfulness. Audiences from all over the world have joined the conversation, seeking one hour of hope for their wavering resilience.

The purpose of World Women's Wellness Day is to remind women that self-care is about self-preservation and to urge all women to make themselves a priority. The free two-day virtual conference, comprising panels, workshops, and more, will provide access to the leaders, specialists, and resources necessary to help women from all backgrounds reevaluate and reshape their lives to affect women's wellness directly.

The first day will kick off with an exclusive keynote from Michelle Robin, DC, on her work, *Small Shifts for Big Impact*; and a reflective, early morning all-level yoga class and tea meditation led by certified yoga practitioner, Melissa Wojcik. This will be followed by several group and individual coaching sessions around a number of wellness and health issues. Speakers over the two days will include Alethia Jackson, VP, federal government relations at Walgreens; Julie Silver, MD, Mass General Brigham; diversity leader and expert Mary-Frances Winters; international wellness advocate Ceasar Fernando Barajas; celebrity attorney Laura Wasser; Cigna's Susan Smith, chief marketing officer, and Stuart Lustig, MD; acclaimed Sleep Doctor Michael Breus, MD; activist and therapist Jasmine Banks; Sodexo executive chef Desiree Neal; and leading nutritionists Afaf Qasem, Cordialis Msora, and Kimberly Wolf-Hagenbuch.

Founder Sheila Robinson, EdD, says, "We want to help transform the lives of women to be healthy, happier, and provide solutions to help them achieve greater success personally, with their children and partners, and in their work life. Our metaphor is 'put your mask on first,' which is what flight attendants tell us. It emphasizes the importance of making ourselves a priority by taking care of ourselves even before taking care of our children. We, as women, don't put our masks on first. We put them on last, which is why our health, happiness, and even wealth are negatively impacted. We want to educate, inform, and transform women by showing them how to put their mask on first, take care of their needs first so they will be *better* mothers, wives, partners, employees, and people."

See the original at www.NationalDayArchives.com

Resources for You at Diversity Woman Media

Diversity Woman Media is the leading multi-platform professional and executive leadership development enterprise and community that advocates for diversity, equity, inclusion, and belonging. Founded in 2015 by Sheila Robinson, EdD, the company provides guidance, training, and mentorship to build our next generation of leaders.

Our nationally recognized portfolio comprises three core areas: publications (*Diversity Woman Magazine* and *Inclusion Magazine*), leadership development academy workshops, and national conferences (including Diversity Woman Digital; the National Diversity Women's Business Leadership Conference; Business Leaders Women in Tech Conference; Inclusion Innovation Leadership Summit; and the Diversity, Equity, Inclusion & Belonging Conference).

Visit our website and follow Diversity Woman Media on Facebook, Twitter, and Instagram. Be sure to view our many resources, including the content from our Moving Forward and Wellness Wednesday webinars.

https://www.diversitywoman.com/

 Diversity Woman – Home | Facebook

 Diversity Woman Media – (@DiversityWoman) / Twitter

 Sheila Robinson – YouTube

About the Author

Sheila Robinson, EdD, is a celebrated publisher, author on leadership, inspiring speaker, and talent innovation specialist. Her company, Diversity Woman Media, is recognized nationally as a leading multi-platform enterprise with program offerings that advance all dimensions of diversity and inclusion (D&I).

Robinson helps leading companies transform their culture to reach gender parity, equity, and belonging by combining her first-hand experience climbing the corporate ladder with the highest academic degrees, best practices from her leading magazines, and a deep passion for evidence-based workplace learnings.

During her fourteen-year career at a Fortune 100 company, Robinson rose from working on the factory floor to the executive office, ultimately directing communications for a $6 billion division of a global chemical company. Her experiences, including the obstacles she faced as an African American businesswoman in the South, led her to want to help other business leaders achieve leadership success in their career journey. Over the past two decades, Diversity Woman Media has grown to become a multi-faceted company that helps customers drive and deliver business results through diversity, inclusion, and talent development initiatives.

Redefining Your Life D.I.E.T.: Transforming How You Look, Feel, and Perform is Robinson's third book. Previous books include *Lead by Example: An Insider's Look at How to Successfully Lead in Corporate America and Entrepreneurship* and *Your Tool Kit for Success: The Professional Woman's Guide for Advancing to the C-Suite*.

Robinson serves with the most influential organizations that are working to foster equity, equality, and inclusive workplaces, including Paradigm for Parity (Advisory Board Member), Catalyst (Strategic Business Partner), Executive Leadership Council (Media Partner), Women's Business Collaborative (WBC – Chair of Diversity), Twitter (Member, Inclusion Diversity Council), and Simmons College Institute for Inclusive Leadership (Board of Advisors).

She holds certificates from Stanford University's Professional Publishing Program, Wharton's School of Business Chief Learning Officer Program, and Cornell University's Diversity and Inclusion Program. Robinson is a Certified Executive Coach and member of the International Coach Federation, the world's largest community of professionally trained coaches.

Dr. Robinson holds a Doctorate of Education from the University of Pennsylvania.

Inspiring, impactful, and practical, Sheila Robinson is moving the world toward gender parity and inclusivity, one woman and one company at a time.

Sources Cited

Chapter 1
Arthur Agatston, MD, and Natalie Greary, *The South Beach Diet Gluten Solution: the Delicious, Doctor-Designed, Gluten-Aware Plan for Losing Weight and Feeling Great—Fast!* (Emmaus, PA: Rodale, 2013).

Tom Rath, *Eat Move Sleep: How Small Choices Lead to Big Changes*, (Arlington, VA: Missionday, 2013).

Chapter 2
Arthur Agatston, MD, and Natalie Greary, *The South Beach Diet Gluten Solution*.

Amelia Nagoski, DMA, and Emily Nagoski. PhD, *Burnout: The Secret to Unlocking the Stress Cycle*, (New York: Ballantine Books, 2019).

Michelle Robin, DC, "Let's Transform Your Life!" *Dr. Michelle Robin*, Jun 2021, http://www.drmichellerobin.com (last accessed Jun 21, 2021).

"Follow the Rainbow to Your Health," *Mayo Clinic Health System*, Jun 2021, https://www.mayoclinichealthsystem.org/hometown-health/speaking-of-health/follow-the-rainbow-to-your-health (last accessed Jun 21, 2021).

David Servan-Schreiber, *Anticancer: A New Way of Life*, (New York: Penguin Books, 2017).

Chapter 3
Brian Keane, *The Fitness Mindset: Eat for Energy, Train for Tension, Manage Your Mindset, Reap the Results*, (Gorleston, UK: Rethink Press, 2018).

Carol S. Dweck and Ant Hive Media, *Carol Dweck's Mindset: The New Psychology of Success: Summary*, (Boulder, CO: Ant Hive Media, 2016).

Chapter 4
Emma J. Bell, *9 Secrets to Thriving: Uncovering Your Inner Resilience*, (Newark, NJ: Audible Studios, 2020), audiobook.

Michelle Brandt, "Snooze You Win? It's True for Achieving Hoop Dreams, Says Study," *Stanford Medicine News Center*, Aug 2011, https://med.stanford.edu/news/all-news/2011/07/snooze-you-win-its-true-for-achieving-hoop-dreams-says-study.html (last accessed Jun 21, 2021).

Benjamin Hardy, "This Morning Routine Will Save You 20+ Hours Per Week," *The Mission*, Aug 2016, https://medium.com/the-mission/how-to-structure-your-day-for-optimal-performance-and-productivity-dcbf0665e3f3#.cmq1lmhw7 (last accessed Jun 21, 2021).

Arianna Huffington, "10 Years Ago I Collapsed from Burnout and Exhaustion, and It's the Best Thing That Could Have Happened to Me," *Thrive Global*, 2017, https://journal.thriveglobal.com/10-years-ago-i-collapsed-from-burnout-and-exhaustion-and-its-the-best-thing-that-could-have-b1409f16585d (last accessed Jun 21, 2021).

Wanda Krause, PhD, "Why Well-Being Has Everything to Do with Productivity," *Medium*, May 2017, https://medium.com/thrive-global/why-well-being-has-everything-to-do-with-productivity-bc89ecc09959 (last accessed Jun 21, 2021).

Caroline Mbaabu, "Effect of Workplace Recreation on Employee Well-being and Performance: a Case of the Commission for University Education (CUE)," *Kenyatta University Institutional Repository*, 2013, http://irlibrary.ku.ac.ke/bitstream/handle/123456789/10165/Effect%20of%20workplace%20recreation%20on....pdf?sequence=1 (last accessed Jun 21, 2021).

Derek Mowbray, "Performance Is All about Wellbeing (sic)," *Training Journal*, 2013, https://www.trainingjournal.com/articles/feature/performance-about-wellbeing (last accessed Jun 21, 2021).

Chapter 5

Jason Fung, MD, *The Obesity Code: Unlocking the Secrets of Weight Loss*, (Vancouver, BC: Greystone Books, 2016).

"Mayo Mindfulness: Laughter for Stress Relief Is No Joke," *Mayo Clinic News Network*, https://newsnetwork.mayoclinic.org/discussion/mayo-mindfulness-stress-relief-with-laughter-is-no-joke/ (last accessed Jun 21, 2021).

Jim Loehr and Tony Schwartz, "The Making of a Corporate Athlete," *Harvard Business Review*, Jan 2001, https://hbr.org/2001/01/the-making-of-a-corporate-athlete (last accessed Jun 21, 2021).

Tom Rath, *Eat Move Sleep*.

Chapter 6

Jason Fung, MD, *The Obesity Code.*

"Water: How Much Should You Drink Every Day?" *Mayo Clinic,* 2017, https://www.mayoclinic.org/healthy-lifestyle/nutrition-and-healthy-eating/in-depth/water/art-20044256 (last accessed Jun 21, 2021).

Cristina Molina-Hidalgo, Alejandro De-la-O, Manuel Dote-Montero, Francisco J. Amaro-Gahete, and Manuel J. Castillo, "Influence of Daily Beer or Ethanol Consumption on Physical Fitness in Response to a High-Intensity Interval Training Program. The BEER-HIIT Study," *Journal of the International Society of Sports Nutrition* 17 (1), https://jissn.biomedcentral.com/articles/10.1186/s12970-020-00356-7 (last accessed Jun 21, 2021).

"MyFastingChallenge—Intermittent Fasting for Weight Management," *My Fasting Challenge,* https://myfastingchallenge.com/ (last accessed Jun 21, 2021).

Jessica Ball, MS, RD, "What Happens to Your Body When You Drink Alcohol?" *Eating Well,* December 19, 2019 (last accessed Aug 23, 2021).

Chapter 7

Rachel Link, MS, RD, "11 Best Healthy Fats for Your Body," *Dr. Axe,* Oct 18, 2018, https://draxe.com/nutrition/healthy-fats/ (last accessed Jun 21, 2021).

Gin Stephens, *Fast. Feast. Repeat.*, (New York: St. Martin's Griffin, 2020).

Sharyn Wynters, "How Toxic Is Aluminum Cookware?" *Cancer Schmancer,* Nov 19, 2013, https://www.cancerschmancer.org/blog/fran/how-toxic-aluminum-cookware (last accessed Jun 21, 2021).

"Microbiome." *National Institute of Environmental Health Sciences,* https://www.niehs.nih.gov/health/topics/science/microbiome/index.cfm (last accessed Jun 21, 2021).

Mindy Pelz, and Bonnie Carlson, "The Reset Factor Kitchen: 101 Tasty Recipes to Eat Your Way to Wellness, Burn Belly Fat, and Maximize Your Energy," *The Resetter Podcast with Dr. Mindy Pelz,* Jul 2021, https://drmindypelz.com/resetter-podcast/ audio podcast (last accessed Jun 21, 2021).

"Think Dirty Shop Clean – Clean Beauty App – Shop Clean Products," *Think Dirty Shop Clean*, Jul 2021, https://thinkdirtyapp.com/ (last accessed Jun 21, 2021).

"Weight Loss: Feel Full on Fewer Calories," *Mayo Clinic*, https://www.mayoclinic.org/healthy-lifestyle/wieght-loss/in-depth/weight-loss/art-20044318 (last accessed Aug 23, 2021).

Chapter 8

Erin Brodwin, "There's Even More Evidence that One Type of Exercise Is the Closest Thing to a Miracle Drug that We Have," *Business Insider*, Jul 2017, https://www.businessinsider.com.au/best-exercise-for-brain-body-2017-7 (last accessed Jun 21, 2021).

Ron Friedman, "Regular Exercise Is Part of Your Job," *Harvard Business Review*, Oct 2014, https://hbr.org/2014/10/regular-exercise-is-part-of-your-job (last accessed Jun 21, 2021).

Stephen Guise, *Mini Habits: Smaller Habits, Bigger Results*, (Seattle: Selective Entertainment LLC, 2013).

"Exercising to relax," *Harvard Health*, Jul 2018, https://www.health.harvard.edu/staying-healthy/exercising-to-relax (last accessed Jun 21, 2021).

Michael Michalko, *Thinkertoys: A Handbook of Business Creativity for the '90s*. Berkeley, CA: Ten Speed Press, 1991).

Tom Rath, *Eat Move Sleep*.

"The 4 Most Important Types of Exercise," *Harvard Health*, Aug 20, 2019, https://www.health.harvard.edu/exercise-and-fitness/the-4-most-important-types-of-exercise (last accessed Jun 21, 2021).

Chapter 9

Rick Hanson and Forrest Hanson, *Resilient: How to Grow an Unshakable Core of Calm, Strength, and Happiness*, (New York: Harmony Books, 2018).

Richard Citrin and Alan Weiss, *The Resilience Advantage: Stop Managing Stress and Find Your Resilience*, (New York: Business Expert Press, 2016).

Emilia Benjamin, Paul Muntner, Alvaro Alonso, et al. "Heart disease and stroke statistics-2019 update: a report from the American Heart Association," *Circulation*, January 31, 2019, Heart Disease and Stroke Statistics—2019 Update: A Report From the American Heart Association | Circulation (ahajournals.org) (last accessed Jun 21, 2021).

"Healthy Eating Plate," *The Nutrition Source*, Jan 2019, https://www.hsph.harvard.edu/nutritionsource/healthy-eating-plate/ (last accessed Jun 21, 2021).

Byron Katie and Stephen Mitchell, *Loving What Is*, (New York: Three Rivers Press, 2002).

David Rock and Daniel Siegel, "Introducing the Healthy Mind Platter," *HuffPost*, Aug 3, 2011, https://www.huffpost.com/entry/healthy-mind-platter_b_870664 (last accessed Jun 21, 2021).

Chapter 10

Arianna Huffington, *The Sleep Revolution: Transforming Your Life, One Night at a Time*. (London: Harmony, 2017).

Jason Fung, MD, *The Obesity Code*.

Elizabeth Hopper, "Your Sleep Tonight Changes How You React to Stress Tomorrow," *Greater Good*, Jul 2021, https://greatergood.berkeley.edu/article/item/your_sleep_tonight_changes_how_you_react_to_stress_tomorrow (last accessed Jun 21, 2021).